"Help! What Do I Do Now?"

"Help! What Do I Do Now?"

The adventures of a young missionary nurse in Vietnam

By Marilyn Faye Bennett

Southern Publishing Association, Nashville, Tennessee

This book was: Edited by Gerald Wheeler
                 Designed by Dean Tucker
                 Cover photos by Emily Timm, Steve Thompson, J. Bruce Baumann/Image
                 Type set 9/12 Helvetica Roman
                 Printed in U.S.A.

2292715

Dedicated to my parents:
Harry and Ercel Bennett

my brother and sister-in-law:
Harry and Marilyn Elaine Bennett

and my niece and nephew:
Bradley and Bonnie Bennett

Special acknowledgments and thanks to my mother for typing the manuscript, to Miss Esther Oldham and Colonel Richard Sessums for the inspiration they gave me while I was in Vietnam, and to Dr. Edna Mae Loveless and Mrs. Virginia Reedy for their suggestions and help in writing the manuscript.

Contents

Foreword

Vietnam is as controversial today as it was during the months and years of undeclared war in Indochina. Political ideologies, military strategy, and economic foibles have all been involved in this Asian nation that captured the attention of America for nearly a decade.

But Vietnam is a nation with millions of people, most of whom have known nothing but war and bloodshed. They long for peace and a better way of life. The gospel of Jesus Christ needs to go to Vietnam just as it needs to go to any other part of the world.

The church can give the gospel message to underdeveloped countries in many different ways. The medical program is one major approach. It brought Marilyn Bennett to Vietnam.

This book relates her experiences in Saigon during the Vietnam conflict. Her assigned responsibility was to organize and direct a school of nursing for the Saigon Adventist Hospital. South Vietnam had no other nongovernment school of nursing at that time.

From headquarters in Singapore, where I served with the Far Eastern Division, I visited Saigon numerous times during Miss Bennett's service in Indochina and observed her association with student nurses at the hospital. One day I went along with the student group as they affiliated with another

Vietnamese hospital in the Saigon area.

Despite her youth, Marilyn had the respect of her students. She was friendly and helpful, yet firm with the program she outlined for the fledgling nurses. With no time for language study, she often found communication barriers in her work.

Since Marilyn was one of the youngest missionaries in the division, with no family there to boost her morale, I deliberately planned time on my Saigon stops to visit her school and counsel with her.

Even though I knew that inwardly she battled problems, she was always effervescent and positive in her hopes for the hospital and the Vietnamese people, especially her student nurses.

Marilyn's story depicts life as it really was at the Saigon Adventist Hospital and the mission housing compound. Pulling no punches, she details the negative as well as the positive, the lows as well as the highs in her overseas assignment. Her frankness is not designed to criticize but to reveal that missionaries are human. The undeclared war added a dimension not conducive to soothe frayed nerves.

When Marilyn's stint in Vietnam ended (we never encouraged single missionaries to remain more than two years in Vietnam), her zest for adventure took her to literally dozens of other countries of the world on her way home. I know of no other American girl who has had the courage to travel as Marilyn Bennett did.

The Adventist involvement in Vietnam's medical program is now ended. The Marilyn Bennett story is a vivid reminder of one of the most exciting periods of my own personal service in the Far Eastern Division.

D. A. Roth,
Associate Secretary,
General Conference of Seventh-day Adventists.

Help! What
Am I Doing Here?

The thundering crash of an explosion broke the stillness of the balmy Vietnamese night. The whole earth shook while the sturdy two-story yellow mission house heaved and swayed. Louvered glass windowpanes rattled in their iron frames.

Automatically I twisted in my bed, then jerked myself into a sitting position. My whole bed jumped up and down in an angry rhythm. Spontaneously I clutched the frames of the iron bedstead, grasping my fingers around the cool metal. The white walls swayed slightly, then stopped. Everything stood still. A hot breeze blew in through the open windows. But a cold chill shivered through my spine. I pulled the light cotton sheet around myself in defense. Wet perspiration streamed down my face.

The sudden silence vanished as another blast rocked the building. Then more explosions thundered in the near distance. The jerking, swaying, and vibrating seemed endless, though it actually lasted only a few seconds. I listened to the helicopters buzzing overhead. The jets from nearby Ton Son Nhut Air Base screamed on into the darkness of the Oriental night.

Myriads of thoughts flooded my mind as I lay back in my bed. Sleep had fled for the rest of the night—I knew that. It was my first night in Saigon. From the descriptions the other missionaries gave, I knew a B-52 bombing raid had started.

Fighting still surrounded Saigon following the devastating offensives against the city just a few weeks before. Reports from the military indicated that Saigon would receive another Communist attack any day now. The entire city lay tense and nervous, wondering when a new siege would begin. The military enforced a strict curfew from seven o'clock in the evening till seven in the morning. Soldiers automatically shot anyone found on the streets during the forbidden hours. So now, during the darkness of the night, the B-52 bombers smashed enemy targets all around the outskirts of the city in an attempt to avert the impending invasion.

I listened to the staccato blasts from the machine guns not far away, then the monotonous "thud-thud" of the outgoing artillery. At times the whole night atmosphere lighted up with the brightness of daytime as flares pierced the sky. Bits of breakaway phosphorus from the flares swished wildly earthward. Occasionally I heard the whine of the incoming Communist rockets. All of it was merely a nightly ritual that one had to learn to tolerate, the other missionaries had informed me.

"Oh, well," I sighed. "Maybe one of these days I'll get used to it and sleep right through like the others." My mind whirled now.

"Help! Oh dear me, whatever am I doing here in all this pandemonium?" I asked myself. "Whatever made me decide to be a missionary to Vietnam anyway?"

Lying quietly now on the hard narrow bed, my mind trailed off ten thousand miles to home. Suddenly I missed Keene, that peaceful little town nestled serenely among the gently rolling plains of central Texas. I longed to be in my own comfortable bed back home, snuggled safely in the neat, white wooden frame house with its dainty leaf-patterned iron latticework and immaculate green lawn.

Never before had I missed my parents so much. I could

almost see my father, with the dash of gray sprinkled
throughout that jet-black head of thick hair. His short frame
always stood straight. He walked with a fast, brisk gait. I
remembered the tears in his eyes when I kissed him good-bye
at Love Field in Dallas—the first tears I'd ever seen my father
shed. Then there was my mother. A dainty, vivacious woman,
she looked young enough to be my sister. Her gentle calmness
stabilized and refined my more daring spirit. My parents were
my best friends. A close tie enveloped our whole family.
Parting had been traumatic.

My reflections continued. I envisioned my older brother,
whom I'd always called Jody. A strong bond dating back to our
childhood had developed between us. Now, Jody's wife,
Marilyn Elaine, seemed just like my own sister. They had also
left the United States for a mission term just a few days before
my own departure. Only they sailed in the opposite direction
from the Orient—Brazil awaited them.

Momentarily I giggled, recalling the multitude of round
packing barrels and square crates all over my parents' house
and yard just a few days before. Some were mine, but most
belonged to Jody and Marilyn Elaine. Each of us attempted to
keep our belongings separate as our practical papa dashed
about madly, trying to get his children packed for their
respective overseas mission assignments. I wondered if
Brazil-bound bundles would arrive in Vietnam and some of my
Saigon shipment would land in South America.

Suddenly my mind stumbled to a halt. Two years was a
long time. I started sobbing in the solitude of the downstairs
guest room in the old yellow mission house.

"You can't cry now," I chided myself. "You *can't* be
homesick. If you're not brave right now, you've got to pretend
you are—you've got to *learn* to be brave."

The din of battle still roared in the near distance. But my
thoughts sailed past Texas to my childhood. Foreign lands

were not new to me. Just before my first birthday, my parents crossed the Atlantic Ocean in a small Portuguese vessel to work in the Belgian Congo. World War II still raged at that time. German submarines infested the ocean, but the family sailed from Philadelphia to Lisbon safely. My folks had a hungry, cold, five-week wait in Lisbon before they launched out on another Portuguese ship to Africa. Portugal sold its surplus crops to Germany, so food became quite scarce. My parents gave whatever food they could buy to three-year-old Jody and me. But we were too young to appreciate their sacrifice. Somehow the family survived by purchasing minute quantities of exorbitantly priced imported canned foods on their meager mission allowance.

From my parents' vivid portrayals later, I knew by heart the description of their landing in the Congo. The tiny Portuguese ship dropped anchor out of sight of land. White-capped waves lashed against the rusty sides of the old boat, tossing it harshly back and forth. The craft sat off the mouth of the Congo River, but it would not venture upstream. Instead, the crew tossed a ladder over the ship's side down to a small open barge. We and our baggage descended the precarious ladder while the ship rolled with the waves which splashed everything with their salty spray.

Leaving the small ship behind, the tiny open barge, which had not even a hint of railing, chugged toward land through the churning currents. My seasick parents clung to us children and each other to keep from hurtling overboard into the turbulent waters. As they sat on their now-battered suitcases, the tropic sun beat down on their bare heads. Perspiration streamed down their faces, finally saturating all their clothes. After several hours they finally spotted land. They shouted for joy, then just sat staring at their destination.

The tiny river town of Banana, sitting on a peninsula jutting into the mouth of the great Congo River, did not welcome the newcomers. The first night all four of us slept huddled together in one bed under the only available mosquito net. The sweltering night atmosphere hung thickly around the mildewing net, making the humid air almost impossible to breathe. But malaria gripped the torrid coast, and my family took every available precaution against the dreaded illness. No one in the area spoke English. My parents knew no native dialects or French then. Because no established Seventh-day Adventist project or institution then existed in that part of Africa, no missionaries met us. My parents journeyed inland alone to their assigned mission station.

We chugged up the Congo River by boat. The ancient craft, a leftover paddle-wheel woodburning steamer, was a relic salvaged from the Mississippi River era and shipped over to the Congo. From the deck my parents watched the swirling whirlpools in the crocodile-inhabited river around them. Looking across to the banks, they observed the tranquil scenes of river life. Little thatch-roofed mud huts stood in clusters here and there, surrounded by tall palm trees. Brown, bare-skinned children scampered underneath in the shade. Bare-breasted women sauntered straight-backed along the river paths, balancing loads of wood and produce on their heads. Brawny men marched along the paths to gardens along the river. Dugout canoes hugged the bank while men fished from them. My father has told me how he often wondered how the message of salvation would ever reach those vast throngs deep in the endless jungles.

Misfortune struck our family as we paddled up through the interior of the Congo. Suddenly my father became acutely ill with malaria. No medical help was available. My mother was frantic with concern over her deathly sick husband as well as with the responsibility, there in the middle of the Congo River, of caring for her two toddlers. But our family survived, in spite of my father's losing twenty pounds. God watched over us.

When we arrived at the point where the giant river is no longer navigable, my parents hired an old battered truck with its African driver to transport us the remainder of the hectic journey. No air or rail service existed in that uncivilized Congolese corner then. The old truck jerked and bumped slowly along the rough, muddy road, which resembled a winding cowpath.

We crossed rivers by pontoon—a ferryboat rig made by tying dugout canoes together and placing planks across them for the vehicle's wheels. The Africans either pushed the craft across with long poles, digging deeply into the water; paddled; or pulled the canoes by tugging at a heavy rope or wire cable strung across the water and tied securely to trees at either side of the riverbank. The polers, paddlers, or tuggers chanted in unison, perspiration standing out all over their powerful black bodies. Although I don't remember those first rides, later I loved crossing rivers by pontoon. Each trip excited me. Sometimes it could be a little frightening. Once the cable broke while a fellow missionary crossed, sending the truck-laden runaway pontoon whirling down the treacherous river. The passengers panicked, knowing the river dropped down a waterfall not far downstream. And I remember how my own family screamed when Daddy nearly lost his truck on one of the hazardous crafts. The pontoon started sinking with the weight of the heavily loaded vehicle right in the middle of a crocodile-infested river.

So I grew up amid the remote mountains and jungles of the eastern Congo in an area known as "Africa's Switzerland," Ruanda-Urundi. My first African home, Rwankeri Mission, rested on a high fertile plateau at eight-thousand-feet elevation. Green terraced mountains and majestic snow-tipped volcanoes surrounded it. Vegetables and fruits grew large and plentiful in the rich volcanic ash. The missionaries had large garden plots and hired full-time native gardeners to tend them.

Unfortunately, the occasional visit of an elephant herd could flatten the tender plants. At times the surrounding villages kept fires burning continously to keep them away.

Once the inhabitants of a nearby village called my father to help them chase the elephants from their gardens. Having no transportation other than his bicycle, he had to ride slowly over the mountains. By the time he arrived at his destination, the enormous beasts lay motionless on the ground, the stench of death permeating the cool, crisp air. The men had already speared them. The villagers, skinning and carving the carcasses, prepared to consume the elephant flesh. Daddy arrived just in time for the festive celebration, but the elephant meat didn't tempt his vegetarian palate.

Sometimes the volcanoes surrounding the area erupted, spewing molten lava into the unsuspecting countryside. Whole villages perished as the sides of the mountain burst open and the thick, glowing lava swept through the land like a giant black and red wave. The mission never evacuated, for the sea of lava didn't reach quite that far. But I remembered stumbling over the hot rocks with Jody after a volcanic eruption. Our little feet sizzled even though the chilly wind nipped our ears. Far below us we could see the bubbling from the molten rocks.

Then we moved to a different location. I remembered life at Ndora Mission well. Our new home sat on a lonely—yet lovely—knoll, encircled by the lofty green mountains of Urundi. Not far from the mission lay a foreboding forest filled with frightening sounds. I recall the eerie noises—soft bellowings, twigs snapping to announce the nearness of some fearful forest beast, the chittering of strange jungle birds, and the chattering of monkeys and baboons swinging in the trees.

Once Daddy became gravely ill. Mother wanted to transport him to Ngoma Mission Hospital, a two-day journey by truck. So our family traveled through the terrifying forest that my four-year-old soul hated. The rain fell in torrents and turned the jungle road into thick brown mud. Gingerly Mother drove the green truck, slipping and sliding it along the narrow road. But soon the truck became stuck. Mother and Jody then decided to strike out through the forest paths to find someone to push us out.

The area was so remote that some tribes living in the forest had never seen a white face. Spellbound I had listened while our African servants told me weird stories about the animals and people inhabiting the jungle. Now, crying with fright, I peered out through the cab window, watching my mother and beloved Jody fade into the gathering dusk of the wet forest. Daddy and I lay silently in the cab. He stretched out on the seat, smothered beneath the blanket, while I sprawled out on the floor, my legs twisted around the gear shift.

As the evening wore on, I continued to lie stiff and rigid, too scared to move as I listened to the sounds around me. The raindrops beat against the window, chanting an eerie rhythm, sending chills sprinting up and down my spine. I kept telling myself to be brave and strong because I must protect and care for my ill father until Mother and Jody returned.

That experience happened years ago. Now I was a supposedly grown woman, but surrounded by the equally foreboding wailing of war. Once again I lay telling myself to be strong and brave.

The loud noises outside my Saigon bedroom continued to remind me of long ago. My thoughts raced back again to my African childhood. I recalled how, during the cool of the night, leopards crept out of the forest, down to the mission. Lying in my bed, I always stiffened with fright as the giant cats coughed outside my bedroom window. Nothing but a screen separated us from them. The leopards routinely killed our chickens. Once they even gnawed my big pet cat, Fluffy, to death. I wept when I found his chewed, half-eaten carcass the next morning just outside the screened window. Often hyenas barked and jackals yelped around the sturdy old red-brick mission house at night. Hearing them outside, I would jump from my bed and run wildly into my parents' room. They would calm me, assuring me that the guardian angels watched over us all. Then I would tiptoe back to bed and fall asleep.

That night in Saigon I remembered how Jody and I arose early in the dewy mornings to play in the vegetable garden. We would usually go to some giant green cornstalks. One morning as we ran down the stony path, a huge shadow leaped across it. Looking closer, I saw the eyes of a leopard staring at us in the dawn. Terrified, we tore breathlessly back up the hill to the house. Strangely, the beast did not follow but slunk away into the thicket.

The safaris with Daddy deep into the interior of the jungles were always exciting. My father frequently traveled around, baptizing new converts or visiting isolated schools and churches. Leaving the truck by the roadside when it became impossible to drive farther, we would walk the rest of the way through the forests, wading through rivers and climbing the mountains. When I grew weary, tall, strong Africans carried me up high on their shoulders. From my perch, my blonde pigtails bobbing on my back, I would reach up and catch the jungle vines hanging down. Sometimes four native porters carried us children in large oval baskets. At night our family slept inside an orange canvas tent and listened to lions roaring in the distance. But I wasn't afraid then—my daddy was near.

By the time I was five, I had conquered my fear of strange noises and animals prowling outside. But the hubbub outside my Vietnam window right now was not comforting. Thoughts from long ago still galloped through my mind as I lay quietly in my bed, waiting for the first streaks of dawn to burst across the sky.

Though Ndora was one of Africa's most isolated missions, we Bennett children lived happily. Boredom never existed there. We seldom played with other children of our own race, for we happened to be the only white people for miles around. It took a whole day of constant driving through the forest to reach the next mission, and travel was both strenuous and expensive, since gasoline brought exorbitant prices. So Jody and I played with the African children almost exclusively during our younger years. Consequently, in our childhood we spoke five languages and dialects in order to socialize with family and playmates.

I longed to identify with my darkskinned playmates. When my mother wasn't looking, I slipped off my dresses and tied plain pieces of cloth from her sewing chest around my frame, then dashed around happily with my African playmates. We climbed trees and played all sorts of fascinating games. Dolls were just too mundane. Besides, my playmates didn't have such toys. Of course at times my attempts at identification went a bit too far, such as the time Daddy sent me away from the table for eating with my hands instead of using forks and spoons. After his scolding, I wailed, "Why won't you let me be like my friends?"

Frequently my persistent mother had to coax and cajole me down from the treetops. Sometimes she had to send the servant up the tree after me with relayed threats of punishment. After he pulled me back to earth, she would attempt to teach me some practical arts of feminine life, such as cooking and sewing. Then she'd set me down at the piano and patiently practice with me.

I sat on my parents' laps by the hour, listening to them describe life in that far-off, somewhat-strange land of America, of which, they said, I was also a part. They told stories about Abraham Lincoln and George Washington and taught me "The Star-Spangled Banner" and other patriotic songs. Also they told me of a phenomenon called electricity that made it possible to have lights all night—even big lights outdoors so people could walk at night. No, most people in America didn't use candles and kerosene lanterns in their homes, my parents explained. Americans kept food cold in white boxes and talked to others far away over black ones called telephones. So many cars rolled through the streets that one could stay up all night and still not see them all, I learned. How different from Urundi, I thought.

Motor vehicles were rare in our remote African hinterland then. Excitement grew when the sounds announced the arrival of a lorry (truck) crawling up the mountain on the new government road below the mission. Jody and I always dashed to the roadside to watch it pass, waving excitedly to the African driver. It seemed strange indeed to think of a place such as America where no leopards or hyenas lurked outside at night, a place where they spoke English and everybody had to wear shoes to church. So my parents worked diligently trying to tame their wild child, attempting to instill American culture on their now thoroughly African girl.

Later my parents moved to Gitwe Mission in Ruanda, a more civilized area, where we associated with other missionary children. There I decided to become a nurse. I observed the birth of babies down at the little clinic. I stood by the hour watching lines of the tall stately Watusi pass slowly by the dispensary window, picking up the pills with their long slender fingers. Some limped in with gaping wounds after a fight or accident. Then I looked on with great interest as the African dresser rolled the long white bandages around the oozing red of their dark skin. Miss Standen, a British nurse, was my idol. The kind, yet efficient, woman patiently explained everything to me. And over at the Ngoma Mission Hospital, Dr. Newbold allowed me to watch surgery, unveiling intriguing physical mysteries to me. Someday, I knew, I would be a missionary nurse.

"Who, Me?
No, Sir. Not I, Sir!"

The giant round moon shimmered a peaceful glow earthward, painting the Texas landscape in silver hues. Yawning, I peered out the window, drinking in the sparkling night. I glanced down at my watch—ten thirty, its hands said. In just fifteen minutes the night shift would arrive. Then I could drive home and hop into bed, I told myself. The signed charts stood in their slots, and I had given the last sleeping medication. The patients seemed quiet now. Working Friday evenings at Johnson Memorial Hospital never seemed to do justice to Sabbath, but the beauty of that particular night permeated the atmosphere with a sacredness.

The report to the oncoming shift was short. Soon I drove home. Once inside the house, I found a note on my bed, penned in Mother's handwriting. I picked it up quickly and glanced over it:

"Marilyn, there is an Elder Duane Johnson from the General Conference here in town this weekend, staying in the guest room at the girls' dorm. He wants to talk to you tomorrow morning before church at the dorm. He says it is important. As you know, Dad and I are leaving now with the academy group for Athens. We will be back Sunday. Have a nice weekend.

"Love, Mommie"

Sleepily I laid it on my dresser and plunged into bed, too weary to give the message a second thought.

The next morning I walked down to Harmon Hall for my mysterious appointment. The day was bright. Birds chirped and twittered in the trees, and a cheerful breeze played around the tip of my short flip. Arriving at the guest-room door, I knocked timidly. A tall, smiling man with bits of gray streaked through his dark-brown hair greeted me. Introductions followed swiftly. We sat in the comfortable chairs the room provided for its occupants and chatted superficially a few minutes.

Then he shifted his position just slightly and said solemnly, "Miss Bennett, would you consider overseas service in Saigon, Vietnam? You would be helping with the school of nursing that we have started in connection with our Seventh-day Adventist hospital there. They need help so much."

Chills started running up and down my spine, even though the warm Texas sun beamed in through the open door. Myriads of thoughts, all jumbled together, raced through my mind.

"Why *me?*" I thought to myself, then quickly answered, "No, sir, I'm too young for that. I've never taught a day in my life. It hasn't been even a year since I graduated from Loma Linda. Surely you need someone more mature and experienced for *that* job."

"Yes, Miss Bennett, that would be best in most situations. But for Saigon we need someone young and adaptable, someone who can adjust easily . . ." I vaguely heard his voice, but my own thoughts absorbed my attention momentarily.

"Yes," I told myself, "maybe someone *like* me, but why *me?* There are hundreds of girls like me. Why, why should they choose me? With so many really outstanding nurses in the United States, surely they don't need little *me.*"

"Miss Bennett, the General Conference has searched for two years. No one is willing to go." The deep voice caught my attention again. His gaze rested on me.

"Wonder where they found out about me?" I mused inwardly, tossing an unruly light-brown curl off my forehead. "I haven't even volunteered for mission service with the GC yet. Sure, someday I'll go to the mission field. But not now! I want my master's degree, lots of good experience, more self-confidence in nursing, and naturally, a husband. No! I won't trek off to the ends of the earth alone. Not me. I'm just not that independent!"

I was single. While I had struggled with the decision to marry rather recently, I just didn't feel quite ready for that step yet. After all, I was just out of college and needed to establish my own identity first.

My thoughts flew on. "But why must I go now? Does God really need *me*? Does He *really* want me to leave my homeland so soon in life, at such an important age, and jaunt off to a foreign, war-torn land all alone? Besides, Jody and Marilyn Elaine have just accepted a call to Brazil. The folks'll be heartbroken losing both of us the same year. Seems to me one person in the family leaving for mission service is enough for now."

In silence I studied the man, then stared out the window for several seconds. Doing God's will; going where His church needed assistance most; making the world a bit better for my having been born—such goals had motivated my life. They had been the purpose for my education. A youthful idealism penetrated my personality. But the church was asking me *now*—not in ten years; not after I had my master's degree, nursing experience, and a husband. Yet the philosophy that personal sacrifices were never too great for God's work had pervaded me since childhood. Hadn't my own parents spent the most productive thirteen years of their lives in Africa? Children reared in foreign missions either have a warm, tender love for overseas service, or they despise it. I felt the former.

Finally I spoke. "Yes, I'll consider it." The man handed me a green self-addressed envelope and an application form. The two of us knelt for prayer.

After I walked out the door that morning carrying the green envelope, I stopped just outside and looked at it. "You don't have to send it in, you know," I told myself. It was Sabbath, and the cloudless blue Texas sky smiled overhead. As I walked over to church, friends waved and called to me, but I merely nodded in response. I slipped into a pew toward the back of the large Keene church where I could be alone, trying to concentrate on the sermon but not hearing a word.

Saigon, Vietnam. Saigon, Vietnam. The words jostled continuously through my brain, stomping out every other sensation. War-ravaged Vietnam. I knew nothing about the land other than that. Somehow the war didn't bother me too much though. My African childhood instilled within me a fearlessness—a dashing love for adventure. Yet outwardly a quiet reserve enveloped me and spilled over into an inner hesitancy. To the casual observer I remained an enigma—daring and quite willing to take risks but outwardly shy and quiet at the same time.

It was the thoughts of professional responsibility that really scared me—not the war especially, even though it certainly was a factor to consider. Rather, I felt too young, too inadequate, too dependent. The only response my mind whispered was: Why, why, why must it be *me?* My thoughts again trailed off into confusion.

After graduation from Loma Linda University School of Nursing, I had returned home to work in Texas hospitals for a while. With my family gone that particular weekend, I trudged home alone to the empty house, deeply absorbed in thought. In the solitude of my bedroom I wept. The implications of the morning conversation poured over me. I knelt and tried to pray, but the words stuck in my mouth. Finally I forced them out.

"God, what do You want me to do? . . . I'm so young, so inexperienced. . . . Is it really You who is calling me? . . . Teaching? You know I'm not qualified yet. . . . The war! . . . Vietnam? . . . Why now, God? . . . Someday, but why now?" The words faltered, then fell to the floor. God seemed so far away. Tears warmed my cheeks. Rising from my knees, I lay on the bed, and running my fingers along the white satin piping on the spread, I gazed off inattentively into space. The frilly white curtains rustled in the gentle breeze blowing in through the open window. Then a little gust of wind caught the cover of my Bible and turned it back, exposing my *Sabbath School Lesson Quarterly* that lay inside the front cover. The wind ruffled its pages. Automatically I reached for the quarterly, still preoccupied with my bewildering thoughts. There at the bottom of a page, a quotation seemed to leap up at me.

"When God commanded Moses to do anything, he did it without stopping to consider what the consequences might be. He gave God credit for wisdom to know what He meant and firmness of purpose to mean what He said; and therefore Moses acted as seeing the Invisible" (*Fundamentals of Christian Education,* p. 346).

"Well, I'm not Moses," I thought to myself. "But maybe that note is speaking to me. Moses didn't want to go back into Egypt either. He felt pretty inadequate himself!" I knelt down by my bed again. "God, if You *really* want me to go to Vietnam, I will, but I'm happy here, and I'm having so much fun. . . . Thank You for Your blessings to me. . . . Please show me that it is Your idea. You've led in my life since the day I was born. I trust You. . . . It's all up to You. Maybe from a human angle I am too young, but You know best. Amen."

As I stood up, a quiet peace filled my mind. I was willing to wait now to see which direction God decided to lead me.

Later I filled in the application blank. The form asked for references, so I wrote the names of a few of the nursing instructors from Loma Linda. Inwardly I told myself, "I *know* they won't let this call go through. They can't possibly recommend *me* for mission service now—maybe in ten years, but surely not now." At Loma Linda, I had been one of the quietest members of my class. Though I enjoyed a wide circle of friends, I was not a leader—either by natural ability or desire. I remembered the time my classmates attempted to nominate me for an office in the Student Nurse Association for California, but I shrank back, terrified with timidity. Neither had I been LLU's brain trust. I had been too busy enjoying life in the extracurricular field to throw myself into diligent study. My grades were just ordinary. In fact, my conscience still pricked me just a bit because I knew I could have done much better.

But who wanted to stay in the dorm studying when she could be out having fun? As a result, I knew that if my instructors had taken a poll at graduation of the person *least* likely to be a leader in nursing or a missionary in her own right, my name would have received the majority of votes. So to myself, I halfheartedly made it a test. If by some miracle my instructors recommended me and felt I was mature enough, I would consider going. Then I relaxed, knowing the improbability of it all. Besides that, I also wanted to talk to other adults wiser than I. If they felt I could make an adequate contribution, that would certainly offer another indication that God wanted me in Vietnam.

Along with the application, I wrote a letter asking the General Conference to find someone more experienced and mature. But if they could not, and if others indicated confidence in me, I would try to do my best. Then I folded the forms, stuffed them into that green self-addressed envelope, sealed it tightly, and dropped it into the slot marked "Airmail" down at the post office.

"You've Got to Be Crazy!"

I'd spent the day water-skiing with the neighbors and had returned home later in the afternoon. As I burst into the kitchen, the aroma of cheese and tomato broiling with onion and mushroom greeted me. "Pizza! Oh goody!" I am known to devour pizza by the plateful. "Mommy, how did you know that I'm in the mood for pizza?"

She laughed softly, wiped her hands on the apron covering her pink dress, and looked at me tenderly. "You're always in the mood for pizza. Glad you're home. Oh, by the way, there's a letter for you from the General Conference. I put the mail on your dresser."

"Well, I wonder what they have to say. It's been only just a few days since I mailed the application." Excitedly I dashed into my room and back, ripping open the envelope, the pizza now forgotten. The letter I read aloud to her.

"Dear Miss Bennett,

"This is an official call from the General Conference . . . Saigon, South Vietnam . . . nurse/instructor . . . two-year term . . . status of a regular missionary. Your references are all very good. We feel you are mature enough and will make a real contribution to the Lord's work in the Far East.

"With Christian greetings,
"D. S. Johnson"

The last words came out in a whisper, and I stood suddenly silent as the enormity of my decision exploded within my consciousness. My voice shook as I looked up from the letter. "Mom, I'm scared now. They *really* want *me* to go. I didn't think the call could actually come through. Since it has, this must be God's will. I have certainly prayed about it, but I'm scared."

"Yes, dear. I know you're frightened, but the whole family has prayed and so have our close friends and neighbors. When you're confronted with a difficult decision, and you pray diligently, the answer always comes. There is no question as to what you ought to do. That's how we felt before we made our decision to go to Africa."

"Mom, I know I must go. I discussed it with several people in whom I have a lot of confidence—Elder Wines, Elder Steiner, Elder Stevenson, Miss Burnett—they all encouraged me to go if the official call came. There's no doubt in my mind now. I'll write Elder Johnson tomorrow."

From that day on we took every opportunity to listen to news of the war situation in Vietnam. On TV we viewed buildings exploding behind streams of Saigon residents fleeing into the streets, caught in the cross fire between the Communist forces and the South Vietnamese. The rubble in the battle-stricken city was clearly visible. Newspaper headlines screamed, "400 Americans Killed This Week in War." "Today Saigon Receives 200 Rockets—1200 Civilians Wounded or Killed." The devastating Communist offensives of 1968 were now in progress in Vietnam. The city of Saigon, previously unscathed by the war, now became a prime target for the Viet Cong offensives.

Friends and relatives started writing me as the news of my mission appointment leaked out. Neighbors telephoned and visited. Some gave comfort and courage, but many took an opposing view. One of my best friends commented, "I've enjoyed your friendship so much during the past years. Why do you have to go out there to Vietnam to be killed now? You've got to be crazy!" Others deplored my utter stupidity at exposing myself to so much danger. Over and over the words came rolling from every direction: "You've got to be crazy!" Naturally, it all upset me to a certain extent, but my natural inclination for adventure kept complete discouragement and terror away. Furthermore, I knew I must go.

Sometimes I wondered where the faith of my friends had fled. Surely if God was calling, He would protect. I wasn't going for the joy of the experience or for my own pleasure. In a way I felt a responsibility for helping to finish the church's mission in a war-torn land.

Preparing to leave did have its enjoyable aspects. For example, I had the fun of shopping, of buying everything I needed for two years. I was not going as a student missionary or on a volunteer basis. As a regular missionary I had the responsibility of maintaining my own household. I didn't have much money for outfitting, having graduated from college so recently. Somehow, though, the Lord stretched my few dollars. I found exactly what I wanted on sale in most cases.

Even the multitude of shots—typhoid, plague, cholera, yellow fever, and every other imaginable kind—was somehow bearable, even though my arms ached for days, it seemed.

Farewell gifts came in from friends. One was a bit unique.

"What do you want for a farewell gift from me, Marilyn?" a pilot friend asked.

"That ride you promised me in the stunt plane," I told him. I had been taking flying lessons a few weeks before, and he had said he would give me a ride in a stunt aircraft at a small airport in another city. So the stunt pilot took me rolling through the blue Texas sky early one Sunday morning. Strapped in tightly, we flew upside down and swooped through loops and crazy eights, laughing all the while. My head hung down and my feet dangled weightlessly above in the small cockpit. Dirt and gravel from the floor rained down in our faces. I have some ridiculous fearlessness within me; naturally, I enjoyed the ride immensely. It was my most memorable gift before my departure for Vietnam.

Then my real test arrived, quite unexpectedly. Just a few days after I accepted the invitation, friends casually introduced me to a young man I'll call Mark, a postgraduate student in one of the large eastern universities. Mark would be receiving his doctorate degree shortly, but he worked as a research assistant for a large industrial complex during the summer. Although I had other friends, Mark soon dominated my social life. I really admired him. He was brilliant, yet human and warm; God-fearing, yet fun-loving.

I did not intend for emotional involvements to develop with anyone before my departure. But a warm, mutual attachment grew between the two of us. During the next few weeks we seemed to get to know each other quite well. Our feelings deepened. As my departure time grew nearer, the more unfair it seemed to go off and leave someone whom I had learned to care so much for. I longed to stay so that we could become better acquainted—he wanted me to. We discussed our dilemma. Mark could not leave because his degree was too close to completion. I could not stay. An inner voice compelled me to go. But questions bombarded me. Why hadn't Mark entered my life just a few days before he did? Why hadn't we met before my call came? Many tense, tearful hours I prayed either for permission to stay or more courage to go. But my conscience signaled only, "Go to Saigon."

Intellectually I realized that we had not had enough time with each other for me to make an objective, lifelong decision right then, even though our fondness for each other had grown, and it seemed as though we should be together. Furthermore, the request had arrived before I met Mark. The church needed me in Vietnam—Duane Johnson had told me no one else would go, though the mission board had searched for two years. Feeling a strong sense of allegiance to my church and its needs, I could not turn my back on it now. I had made a promise. Yes, I must go.

But my emotions continued to ache. Bowing my head in reverence one evening, I sobbed, "God, You know the desires of my heart. You know what is best for me. If it is Your will, the relationship with Mark will last through the next two years while we are apart. If not, then You will provide other happiness for me, and You will have some better plan for Mark. I will trust You. I will still go where You lead, but please give me more strength right now. Amen."

Up to now my love for God had been rather naive, a bit immature, quite idealistic, and mostly untried. It had had no real opportunity for it to grow rich and deep through conflict and heartache. My present agony was a spiritual learning experience for me, and Mark admitted that the trauma was bringing him closer to his Maker as well.

But even though I trusted God, the gnawing pain still throbbed deep inside. Mark later wrote me that he also had wept, something he had not done since childhood.

Then one night I stood in my yard and watched Mark drive his green Mustang Fastback into the darkness—out of my life for the present, perhaps forever. The next morning a jet would whisk me away from Texas. So we had just said our good-byes. Intently I looked down the road at the disappearing vehicle. It turned a corner and vanished. Only the thick night stared at me in empty silence. Slowly I trudged toward the house. My arms still ached from the inoculations, and I felt waves of fever surging through my body. In addition, my head throbbed, my stomach churned wildly, and feelings of nausea welled up within—all side effects from that last painful typhoid injection. But along with the burning, I perceived sharp, cold pangs of loneliness. Weeping bitterly, I felt empty, momentarily sorry for myself. But the decision had been my own. Vietnam had been my choice because I was convinced that it was what God had directed. Therefore, I must bravely accept its consequences, whatever they might be.

I looked up into the star-studded sky. Strangely, my thoughts turned to Abraham, to his experience in following God wherever He led, in his dilemma over whether to sacrifice Isaac. They had been excruciating problems to him. But God had provided an alternate for Abraham. At that instant I felt my sacrifice was too great. There was no "ram in the thicket" for me that dark, humid Texas evening. A quotation came to mind: "Those who accept the one principle of making the service of God supreme, will find perplexities vanish and a plain path before their feet" (*The Ministry of Healing*, p. 481).

Yes, I would trust God.

The next day I kissed my parents a tearful good-bye at Dallas Love Field and boarded the waiting American Airlines jet, alone. I wept for two hours solid—the time it took to fly to Los Angeles. Silently I asked God for strength to resist the almost overwhelming urge to take the next plane back to Dallas on my arrival in Los Angeles. After a quick stop in California to bid adieu to friends and former classmates, I again left by myself. In a certain way I felt grateful to be traveling alone. I needed time to think.

So, I, Marilyn Bennett, a shy but adventurous part-child-part-woman, left the security of the United States, the land of my birth and home of all I held dear, and headed for the uncertainties of a country engulfed in war. From an objective standpoint, I was too green, too inexperienced, too youthfully idealistic, too sensitive, perhaps too much of a woman for the "masculine" job and pile of problems awaiting me on the other side of the world. It was good I didn't realize what lay waiting for me then. But the jet flew on into the clear-blue peaceful sky, its innocent passenger fastened securely within, believing fervently she followed the biddings of her Creator.

The first stopover was Hawaii, where friends gave me a gracious welcome in the charm of the Pacific tradition, including leis. Then on to Tokyo, Japan. As I entered the terminal building of the Tokyo International Airport, the foreign atmosphere crashed in around me. All the signs bore Oriental script—completely undecipherable to my Occidental eye. Nowhere did I see so much as one English word—not even one word written in the Western alphabet. Those African dialects I had learned long ago did not help now.

Yet the strangeness held excitement, and I hurried on, following the teeming crowds blindly, but miraculously coming up at the right place. Next I had stopovers in Korea, Taiwan, the Philippines, and Hong Kong. Even though I knew no one personally at these places, someone from the Seventh-day Adventist missions always met me. They treated me as if we were longtime friends. Some of them expressed joy at seeing someone so young with the courage to go to the world's boiling pot—Saigon. It brought them new courage, they told me.

I was thankful they felt that way. If my coming inspired the more experienced, then it softened the heartaches of the good-byes. One motherly woman took one look at me and with a sadness in her voice quietly said, "My, how your mother must have hated to see you go."

Aboard each flight, the subject of destinations came up often with my seatmates. They stared at me in total disbelief when I told mine—Vietnam. Some passengers looked at me with astonishment and blurted out, "You must be out of your mind. You've got to be crazy. Aren't you scared to death?" The passengers held up the newspapers passed out on all flights, pointing to the blaring headlines—"Saigon Bedded Down for Third Offensive!"

On the flight from Taipei to Manila, I sat alone, staring out the window into the blue sky and white clouds zipping by, absorbed in my thoughts. Suddenly a deep voice broke into my solitude.

"Saw you sitting here and thought I'd come chat a few minutes. Mind if I sit beside you?" Before I could answer, the body containing the voice started folding itself nearly in half, squeezing into the seat, his knees jammed up against the one directly in front. His chestnut-brown hair fell in loose waves over his ears, just touching the tip of the wide collar on his red shirt. Smooth yet sinewy hands rested heavily on the sharp crease of his immaculate white trousers, flattening it slightly. He stretched his long neck way back on the headrest and looked over at me. "What's a young lady like you doing traveling the Orient alone?"

"Oh, I'm a missionary," I replied as I shuffled my feet and fidgeted, digging my nails tensely into the clenched palms of my hands. The man ignored my nervous movements.

"You—a missionary! Well—but—you just don't look like one—you—you're too young. Besides—well—guess you're just too well dressed for that!" His brown eyes filled with astonishment, then squinted as the sun beamed in at him.

"Why do you say that? Can't missionaries dress nicely? These are plain ordinary clothes anyway," I replied. Feeling the warmth of a blush rising in my cheeks, I smoothed a natural fold in my bright yellow polyester dress and fumbled with the hem of the skirt, which rested just a bit above the knee. I always seem to blush when men make personal comments to me.

"Yeah, I guess so—guess missionaries can look decent—just never thought about it. It's just that I think of missionaries as being old fuddie-duddies, certainly not modern little ladies!"

"Where did you get that idea?"

"Well—um—guess from my childhood—my folks were Methodist missionaries in Africa—in the Belgian Congo—guess

that's just what I remember. Mission life——" He tried to
continue, but I abruptly interrupted him.

"Missionaries in the Congo! What part?" My hands lay still
now, and I felt a look of interest sparkling from my eyes.

"Oh, you've never heard of the place. Just a little Belgian
mining town in the southeastern part—Katanga
Province—Jadotville. Just what makes you so interested in
that?" His tanned brow furrowed quizzically.

"Sure. I've heard of Jadotville. In fact, we used to go
through there on the train from Elisabethville to Kamina."

"What on earth were you doing in the Congo? Wow! You
do get around, young lady!"

"My folks were missionaries in the Congo too—we lived in
Ruanda-Urundi and Elisabethville. We are Seventh-day
Adventists. Have you ever heard of them?"

"Yes, I have somewhere—don't know too much about
them." The voice trailed off, then came back forcefully, "By the
way, *Parlez-vous Français?"* (Do you speak French?)

"Oui, monsieur, un peu, et vous?" (Yes, mister, a little, and
you?) My interest level really rose now.

"Moi, aussi. [I do too.] Wow! What a coincidence that we
should meet here on this flight. We probably lived about two
hundred miles apart back in Katanga. Really it is a small world,
isn't it? Say, just where are you going on your mission
assignment anyway?" A smile played around his mouth, his
bushy eyebrows lifted in patient expectation.

"Saigon, Vietnam. And where are you going?"

"Saigon! Little lady, you've got to be crazy. Are you for
real? You're too delicate—you just don't look the type." An
expression of utter amazement burst out all over his face. His
heavy jaw hung slightly open in disbelief.

"Hush! Don't say that. I'm sick and tired of hearing people
tell me that." I laughed. "Yes, I'm *really* going to Saigon. Now
how about yourself?"

"Well, believe it or not, I'm going to Saigon too. But I sure didn't think there would be any dames like you there." I felt the warmth of that first blush creep on down my neck. The young man continued, "Guess there'll be some army nurses, but not——" The voice stopped momentarily. "But the war? You—you're not afraid?" The astonished gaze turned to a matter-of-fact look toward me. His tone calmed. "Yeah, I'm a correspondent for *Newsweek*—been with them for two years now—ever since I got my master's from Purdue in journalism. But this is my first overseas assignment. What are you going to be doing in Saigon?"

"I'm a nurse. I'll be working with our Adventist hospital."

"How about that! A real live missionary nurse to Vietnam. Guess they need a few nurses all right, judging from the reports of all the fighting and stuff during these offensives." His voice mellowed. "I really admire you; you don't have to go. Of course I don't either, but I'll be making big pay. It'll be worth my while—war correspondents do quite OK. But you won't. You're going because you really want to do something for your church—something for humanity. You know, I wish I could be dedicated like that. My folks——" His voice trailed off into silence. He looked intently at me for a moment, a softness beaming in his eyes. Then he stared out the window, preoccupied, a penetrating expression covering his face.

Suddenly the jet lunged, beginning the descent to Manila. The fasten-seat-belt sign flashed on, and the tall man rose spontaneously to return to his assigned seat. Standing in the aisle, he leaned over and spoke to me again.

"Say, little lady, where're you staying tonight? I'd like to see you some more. Maybe we could go out for dinner or something. I hear Manila is a swingin' city—plenty of nightclubs. We could really 'groove on out.' " For a moment his voice fell. "Oh, but you're a missionary." He slapped his tanned hand against the head of the seat, a slight tinge of disappointment lurking in his eyes. Then his voice picked up cheerfully: "Well, how about it? Dinner at least?" The man grabbed the back of the seat to balance himself as the jet plunged again.

"Thank you, but I'll be at our mission tonight. They'll be at the airport to meet me. Otherwise I'd gladly join you for dinner." I smiled in return.

"Surely has been fun talking with you anyway. See you in Saigon." The man walked back to his seat, tucking the red shirt neatly back into the waist of the spotless white trousers. The plane continued the descent, landed with a thud, and the passengers filed out to the terminal building.

My courage held up fairly well till the time came for my last flight. I was in Hong Kong. It seemed as though my feet turned colder and colder by the hour. I changed my reservations to the last flight of the day from Hong Kong into Saigon. It was Friday, and I needed to reach Saigon by Sabbath. Ten days had elapsed since I left the States. Homesick, just a bit lonely, and frightened now, I was ready to fly back to Texas. In fact, I felt willing to give everything I owned at that point for permission from my conscience to take the next flight home. But it was too late to back out now.

The missionaries took me to the Hong Kong International Airport. I started crying then, and I didn't stop till I reached Saigon. After I went through customs at the Hong Kong airport, someone directed me to the Air Vietnam waiting area. When I looked around, I discovered to my dismay that I was the only woman in the whole place. American servicemen waiting for their return R and R (rest and recreation) flights back to Vietnam completely surrounded me.

The tears began streaming faster and faster. Seeing all those American men staring at me was almost more than my timid soul could bear. (I was probably the first American woman they had set eyes on in a good long while.) Somehow I felt trapped. The emotions of the past months poured forth in great loud sobs. Now I was so embarrassed that I would gladly have given anything for a hole to crawl into. The situation did have an element of humor—the expressions on the faces of the homesick GI's watching me pour out their sentiments, most likely, about returning to Vietnam. But because I was a woman, society allowed me to express the real feelings evident in the airport that afternoon. I knew they wanted to cry—I saw it written on their faces—but they couldn't. That moment I was grateful to be a woman.

The two-hour flight to Saigon from Hong Kong was uneventful. Eagerly I peered out the window, watching for the first signs of my new homeland. Soon they appeared, nothing but long streaks of green jungle. It was beautiful from thirty thousand feet, and I wondered what it really would be like. But I did not have too long to wait—the giant bird quickly made its descent to Ton Son Nhut Air Base. Looking out the window, all I saw were long lines of various types of planes—fighter jets, ugly multicolored transport planes, and sleek silver bombers.

Descending the Air Vietnam stairway from the jet, I walked slowly toward the terminal. The gentle warm wind ruffled my hair. I felt as though a daze enveloped me—nothing seemed real. Brushing my tears away, I forced myself to smile. This was Vietnam—my new home. "But help! What do I do now?" I asked myself.

The ride to the mission was short but revealing. To my delight I saw only a few bombed buildings. I had expected to see everything in rubble, with rockets exploding constantly and soldiers frantically running to and fro. Life seemed quite normal. Graceful pedestrians sauntered down the dusty sidewalks. Sputtering pedicabs sped in and out of the traffic. Jerking jeeps jumped through the long lines of vehicular confusion. I was so relieved that I nearly cried—for joy this time. Life would be bearable.

What Do
I Do Now?

I stood in the hospital courtyard scanning the surroundings.
The three-story dirty yellow building bearing the sign Saigon
Adventist Hospital stood squashed up against the black iron
fence that separated it from the teeming intersection of two of
Saigon's main thoroughfares. The church jammed up tightly
against the side of the hospital business office, and the wall of
the Adventist Press touched the rear hospital wall. Then, out in
the middle of the courtyard squatted the tiny yellow morgue.
But a small spot of green grass bordered by a row of dainty
pansies in the far corner by the church provided a touch of
beauty.

The courtyard seemed so pressed together that I felt
twinges of geographical suffocation. Coming from Texas, I was
accustomed to gazing out across miles of uninterrupted space
that gave me a contented free feeling. In an attempt to relieve
my claustrophobia, I glanced down the street. Giant
chuckholes blotched the pavement. Dismal rows of shanty
shops huddled side by side or wedged in between junky
military buildings. Beer cans rolled away from garbage piles
that littered the street. The recent fighting within the city had
left the trees barren and gaunt, skeletons pointing their bony
fingers skyward. But, above the crowded streets and city,
clouds graced the blue sky. The bright sun humored the

dejected environment. As I looked up into its peacefulness, the realization faintly dawned on me that I *could* find happiness and beauty anywhere, if I looked for it—yes, even in war-torn Vietnam. Many times in the months that followed, I completely forgot or stubbornly refused to admit that fact, but eventually it would find its way back, and I would discover joy once again.

Suddenly the ground beneath me started shaking. Spinning around dizzily, I grabbed the iron fence to steady myself. The morning sun hit me squarely in the eyes. Squinting, I peered between the rods of the fence. A military convoy of monstrous green ten-ton trucks roared by, dust swirling from behind the gigantic wheels. Truck after truck thundered past, continuously blaring their shrill air horns and exhaling thick black smoke. They carried machine guns, tanks, and huge brown wooden boxes. I soon learned that all the military traffic between Ton Son Nhut Air Base and Long Binh Army Post, the largest camp in Vietnam, passed by our hospital.

Crushed in between the military traffic, there scrambled rickety blue and white taxis, clanking decrepit civilian trucks, and swarms of motorcycles and cyclos,* all trying to arrive first, yet getting nowhere because of being trapped in the massive traffic jams.

Directly overhead several helicopters flew so low they nearly clipped off the tops of the surrounding buildings. Then above the helicopters, giant jets screeched in their holding patterns around Ton Son Nhut Air Base only a couple of miles away. (At the time Ton Son Nhut held the record as the busiest airport in the world for the number of landings and takeoffs. So it was probably similar to having a hospital on the edge of Kennedy International or Chicago's O'Hare.)

Stepping inside the building, I heard everyone talking loudly, sometimes shouting to be heard above the outside din.

---

*A form of local transportation involving a motorcycle with a seat on the front.

It was impossible to carry on a normal conversation, much less hear blood pressures and apical pulses (heartbeats).

In spite of the continual commotion, the sick thronged into the hospital compound, teeming through the iron gates, pushing and shoving their way into the crowded courtyard and on into the small, packed waiting room. Here the people huddled together on long wooden benches or lay on canvas stretchers until the doctors could see them. The waiting room served as an overflow ward when the other areas of the hospital filled up. Then the outpatients sat on the floor or stood pressed in together while hospital patients filled the wooden benches. At times, bottles of intravenous fluids hung precariously from the louvered glass windowpanes, since the hospital never had enough rickety IV poles to go around. Under the wooden benches sat bedpans, a taunting reminder of the total lack of privacy. Some days the waiting room and hospital grounds were so jammed that one had to push and shove his way through.

The building had never been designed as a hospital. It was actually an old French mansion. Though ingeniously remodeled, at its best the structure offered only a mere semblance of efficiency or comfort to either patients or staff. A narrow circular stairway climbed gracefully up the center of the building, maintaining the only means of traffic or communication between the three floors. The staff had to manipulate all patients, equipment, and supplies for the upper floors up and around the steep staircase.

When patients couldn't walk, orderlies or relatives carried them in their arms up the stairs. Sometimes the hospital used canvas stretchers to transport patients. But the tight squeeze around the corners of the staircase made it necessary to tip the stretcher at such an acute angle that the attendants had to hold the patient to keep him from tumbling off. Looks of terror frequently filled the patients' eyes as they precariously rode up and down the winding staircase. Sometimes in their haste to get the patients down the stairs, the orderlies and others rushed them down headfirst, and with their tight grasp they inadvertently pulled the pajama bottoms a bit too far.

Technically the hospital had thirty-eight beds, but most of the time it contained between fifty and sixty inpatients. The extra patients lay on green canvas stretchers in the narrow halls, on top of work desks, in the offices, and jammed side by side in the wards. Occasionally two occupied the same bed. At times conditions were so crowded the nurses could not walk forward down the halls. Instead, they slipped along sideways to keep from bumping into the stretchers or stepping into the bedpans.

The one lone operating room served also as the delivery room. However, if the arriving fetus decided to make its entrance at a time surgeries were in progress, the staff delivered the infant in the hall on a stretcher behind a white cotton screen, with the excited relatives or curious onlookers peeping around occasionally. Following surgery or delivery, two or three attendants again carried the patient up the winding staircase or around the narrow corner to his room. Frequently the surgeon picked the patient up in his own arms while others came along behind holding the catheter drainage bottles, IV's, and sundry tubes.

Although equipment and medical supplies were sometimes sparse, the United States Army handed over obsoletes, surpluses, and duplicates quite generously. I often chuckle as I remember some of the items the U.S. military gave us—four hundred toilets, a truckload of Johnson's baby powder and lotion, and an enormous supply of frozen pizzas on one occasion. The medical director announced to the nursing students he had a special treat for them that evening. They had never tasted pizza before and didn't have quite the relish for it that we American missionaries had. It was all they could do to politely nibble a few bites as they tried our "delicacy." That night around midnight they woke up the cook and implored her to boil a pot of rice for them. The next morning they courteously greeted us: "Please, no more pizza—we no like—the stomachs have sickness in the night."

Meanwhile, physicians from the Third Field Army Hospital down the street from our mission compound frequently gave assistance when their own casualty lists were low.* We cleaned all disposable items, including needles and syringes, and used them time and time again. Empty IV bottles, preciously guarded, functioned as water pitchers or collecting containers for urinary catheter drainage. Used IV tubing found roles as drinking straws, hypodermic-needle covers, oxygen tubing, or catheter drainage. Every patient received a daily bed bath and lay on fresh linen in the morning. But if it became soiled during the course of the day, we could seldom replace it—we had no extras. We did put sheets of brown wrapping paper or newsprint over the soiled areas so the patient could keep reasonably clean. During monsoon seasons (rainy seasons) it was sometimes difficult to get the linen dry for the next day's use. But even during the rains, the sun usually managed to peek through long enough sometime during the day to dry Saigon Adventist Hospital linen.

Clean linen and baths daily were not a part of routine procedure for other Vietnamese hospitals, I soon learned. In Vietnam everyone did the best he could with the situation he had to work with.

The mission compound was located about a mile away from the hospital. It embraced the missionaries' homes, a nine-hundred-pupil secondary day school, the nursing school, houses for national workers, and the servicemen's center. Unlike the rest of Saigon, the "compound," as we affectionately

---

*The military lent its large, well-equipped hospital to our church in January, 1973.

called it, was spacious. The buildings were not all jammed in together. An expansive green lawn bordered by leafy palms and red-flowering tropical trees stretched out between the buildings.* The Vietnamese gardener groomed the grounds carefully, so we felt a pride for our mission that we couldn't always muster up for our ill-located hospital.

But the noise level was not a great deal less than at the hospital. Multitudes of helicopters whirred raucously overhead, frequently interrupting our conversations. We heard that since the compound lawn provided the largest patch of green in the city except for the presidential palace and zoo grounds, the helicopter pilots used it as a guide in navigating. No wonder the choppers flew so low.

Our mission was situated even closer to Ton Son Nhut Air Base than the hospital. It sat on a main street—the same as the presidential palace. Since the military convoys did not pass by our gate with their blasting air horns and nauseous gas exhausts, we felt quite blessed in that respect.

An eight-foot brick wall, broken only by an iron gate continuously manned by a guard, completely surrounded the grounds. We called him the guard, but maybe he should have been named the "gate-sitter" since he merely opened and closed it for us when we wanted in or out.

During the time of the Tet offensives within the city, fighting started right outside the mission gate. The poor frightened gatekeepers pushed the compound gates wide open and fled in terror. I never blamed them for that; perhaps I'd have done the same thing. The angels must have taken over, because no damage occurred to our mission, and the VC never invaded the premises, though I'm told they had once overrun much of the surrounding area.

---

*It later became the site of the partially constructed new Seventh-day Adventist hospital.

Anyway, the gatemen found a special place in my heart. They were such charming little men, with wispy beards composed of just a few strands of long hair. Playful smiles always danced around their brown eyes. Sometimes I just wanted to run up and squeeze them. Of course I managed to control such an impulse, for after all I was the "missionary nurse."

A number of surprises awaited me as soon as I arrived in Vietnam. No one had told me that I would direct the nursing school. Somewhere the administrative process of my church had picked up some misinformation about my qualifications. And besides that, not only was I to be the director, I was supposed to establish and develop the whole nursing school. I couldn't have felt more helpless.

My first year out of college, I was not prepared either professionally or psychologically for the responsibility of creating and administering a nursing school. I had never taught a day in my life.

At that moment I felt that someone had exploited my youth and willingness to serve. Was my church taking advantage of naive, idealistic me? Inner rumblings of anger surged as I wailed outwardly to the man confronting me with my unexpected responsibility, "You can't do this to me. Nobody told me I had to start the school. If I'd known this, I would never have come. Just who do you think I am anyway?" Then to myself I mumbled, "They're wanting a combination of Einstein and Florence Nightingale."

Silently I grumbled to God. "Help, Lord! What am I doing here? What on earth did You bring me here for anyway? What do I do now?" But I didn't wait for Him to answer.

I expressed my feelings of inadequacy in an outburst to my fellow missionary. But at the same time I felt that he, at least twenty-five years my senior, could not be expected to remember the trepidations of youth. In fact, it seemed to me

that his poised self-assurance probably seldom entertained
self-doubt such as I struggled with at that moment. His closing
remark scared me momentarily: "Marilyn, there is no one else
to do it. . . . If you don't, you're not worth the money it took to
bring you out. After all, this is the mission field."

I tried to choke down the lump in my throat and fight back
the stinging tears in my eyes. Quickly my pride forced them
back. But at that point, a desire to lash back nearly overcame
my fright, and I almost let two teardrops fall as I tried to control
my feelings. Later I learned to respect this man deeply even
though we passed through much trouble together. My quiet
hesitancy tried him just as greatly as his professional
aggressiveness aggravated my sensitive, faltering spirit. He
had high goals for me, so my lack of assertiveness frustrated
him. Yet some of the lessons he taught me I shall always
remember, and I now can appreciate his help to me and his
tolerance for my immaturity. He had gifts that helped him
function in a highly charged atmosphere. I esteem him highly,
and we remain friends.

Most of my fellow missionaries were old enough to be my
parents. I happened to be the only single person in the Saigon
mission family, a factor which I did not always view as a
blessing. Some of my co-workers regarded me with an icy
coolness, their feelings mirrored on their faces in "Why-
did-the-General-Conference-send-out-this-infant?" expressions. The fact that the so-called younger generation
had potential definitely awaited demonstration to them. Since
no one else appeared on the scene to prove it, I knew I had
to be the one, whether or not I liked the idea. I never claimed
to be the epitome of maturity or creativity, and I longed for
a dependent, noninvolved role. But God did not see fit to grant
it to me during my term in Vietnam. Instead, I learned to
cope.

On top of the staggering professional responsibilities

heaped on me, I realized that I'd inadvertently stumbled into another difficult situation. Under Saigon's wartime conditions, everyday frictions erupted in alienated feelings and shattered human relations. The emotional atmosphere on the compound seemed thick and black. I found myself in the middle, caught in the cross fire of clashing personalities—one group pushing me, the other pulling just as hard in the opposite direction. Being a newcomer, and a naive one at that, it seemed as though I was chained to the center of the conflicting views. The compound was too small to avoid entanglement. Because of my age, both groups of the missionaries expected me to follow their advice, and they gave me verbal rebuffs if I didn't accept their constantly conflicting counsel.

Looking back on the situation, I do not blame them. We were all so human. When viewed individually, each was a talented, hardworking Christian. Each was a fearlessly courageous person who loved God in his own unique way. And each had definite ideas of how The Work should progress best. The factors that made them outstanding missionaries caused some of the dissension, for only forceful, confident, dedicated people would willingly accept difficult assignments such as Saigon in 1968 following the Viet Cong offensives. (I was the reluctant exception.)

Also, the strain on exhausted nerves caused by the uncertainties of the war was clearly evident. The gigantic work loads during that time exhausted any reserve of physical and emotional energy. Now my youth and inexperience became a part of the problem. In time the war, coupled with overwork, took its toll.

Often I felt sorry for myself as I evaluated my predicament those first days in Saigon. Here I sat, my first year out of college. I was ten thousand miles from home and, as I later learned, the youngest person in the history of the denomination to direct a nursing school, much less to be responsible for establishing one. Outside the mission compound a controversial war made physical life hazardous, and inside I was enmeshed in a tangled web of human relationships. No wonder I feared for my psychological survival.

Over and over I complained to God, "Why did You bring me here? What do I do now? Help! What on earth am I doing here? . . . Are You sure this is what You had in mind?"

And God understood my frustrations. At times the temptation to take the next plane home nearly overwhelmed me. But somewhere a spark of dauntlessness concealed deep within me unearthed itself, and I refused to allow myself a perhaps ungraceful exit from the seemingly impossible task. I believed God led in my life, therefore in my coming to Vietnam. Again and again He gave me faith to believe that He would see me through.

However, lest some misunderstanding arise, let me say that I by no means founded Saigon Adventist Hospital's nursing school. Back in 1955 the hospital first opened its doors to the people of Vietnam. At that time the majority of the nurses came from Adventist nursing schools in the Philippines and Thailand. As it became more difficult to obtain nurses both within and outside the country, the necessity for setting up a training program right at the hospital became glaringly apparent. A wife of one of the early doctors started the first nursing class. When she left Vietnam, the school shut its doors. An Australian nurse, who also had complete charge of the hospital nursing service as well, reopened the school a couple of years later. At the end of her term, the school again closed. Never had there been any ongoing accredited program; never a building, library, or textbooks. The students spent much of their time in on-the-job training, and classroom instruction was somewhat minimal since they never had a full-time person available for nursing education. It was impossible to man the hospital except through our own graduates, since only one other nursing school existed throughout the country, and the Vietnamese government hospitals gobbled up its graduates. Saigon needed a nursing school.

Now the Adventist hospital and mission endeavored to inaugurate an accredited program that would continue indefinitely. The third attempt at nursing education was to be largely my responsibility. Four months prior to my arrival, two of the mission doctors' wives, who also were nurses, had set up a skeleton curriculum and started the first class. But the women were involved with too many other responsibilities to direct the program. Now I needed to amplify the three-year curriculum in detail, develop courses, write guidelines, take over the nursing instruction, and generally manage the total scholastic program. It was a massive order for a first-year graduate. Bewilderment and sheer terror nearly overwhelmed me. Besides, there existed no textbooks, no library, no anatomical models, no teaching aids.

I certainly did not view myself as an efficient leader capable of coming up with answers to difficult situations. In my immaturity I often faltered in seeking the most workable solutions. Consequently I made countless mistakes in judgment. But I could do only what I felt was right after receiving the guidance available. At times I felt as though I stood alone in the midst of a raging turmoil. Yet I survived.

Beginning a
Nursing School

The two-story barracks stood off to itself in a corner of the
compound. It would house the nursing school. The rooms
upstairs served as the dormitory, while the downstairs
contained the library, office, and classrooms.

One of the mission doctors had negotiated with the Navy
Seabees for the construction of the barracks, since the budget
contained no money for new buildings. Even if building funds
had existed, most of the Vietnamese men found themselves
inducted into their army, and local civilian contracting help was
difficult to obtain.

A fellow missionary persuaded the Navy men to erect the
barracks by supplying them with homemade pies and cakes,
baked by the simultaneous efforts of his wife and servant. I felt
grateful that they had finished the baking prior to my arrival,
because I fear my cakes would not have inspired the Seabees.
We'd still be waiting for the nursing school.

The outer shell to the barracks stood complete, and the
plumbing functioned adequately. But the finishing touches such
as painting, laying the floor, and installing electrical wiring
appeared to await my ingenuity to complete.

My talents certainly do not include construction in any form.
But I managed to persuade some of the Adventist GI's to come
to my rescue. That proved to pose a great problem, too, for

their only legitimate reason to come to Saigon was for church on Sabbath. Otherwise military regulations bound them to their bases. Saigon was officially off limits for all American soldiers unless stationed within the city. Most of the Adventists found themselves situated on distant bases. But, bless their hearts, some of them found excuses to come to Saigon during the week to help. Whether or not their reasons found logic with their officers, I never checked. Finally, two coats of donated "army green" paint covered the exterior of the wooden barracks, and the rough beams of the interior gleamed in white. A doctor's wife joined the nursing students in swinging paintbrushes. She also worked many long, sweaty hours helping lay tile in the four classrooms. At times we laughed as we became stuck to the tile glue. To help pass the time, we made jokes about everything imaginable. And to my enjoyment she gave me lots of advice on my romantic life.

While the building wore its coat of army green, one of the Vietnamese Adventists came to me and politely indicated his desire to have a chat. Obligingly I turned from my work to listen. "Miss Bennett, in old Vietnamese legend, a green house is a bad house—a house of ill repute—all nursing students living here—maybe not so good."

"Oh help, what do I do now?" I laughed inwardly while outwardly attempting to remain composed. Some time later we finally finagled several gallons of gray paint from the air force and managed to redo our decor—for the sake of reputation. But the building needed a fresh paint job by then anyway.

One day, in an attempt to finish things up for the school, I desperately struggled to saw boards for bookcases. Now my carpentry ability is rather puny, to be quite generous, but when things need to be done and I can't find capable persons to do them, I've brainwashed myself into believing that my efforts are better than nothing at all—sometimes. So I stood out in the middle of the compound lawn, sawing frantically, but accomplishing nothing even resembling bare minimal quality. The compound gate stood open just enough so that an American serviceman walking by our premises looked in to see my predicament. Gallantly rescuing me, he sawed the boards skillfully.

The barracks-turned-nursing-school now stood ready for occupancy. One of the missionary wives made curtains, and as the white nylon material fluttered next to the screens, the whole building seemed vibrant with a tidiness that made me more than a tiny bit proud. That tidiness was short-lived because of the devastating mixture of dust and monsoons, but one couldn't let minor details deter momentary happiness. It's debatable as to who seemed more excited—the students who moved in or the missionaries who helped prepare the building.

There existed only one problem now—no electricity. We furnished the students with a supply of candles, but the safety factor left that plan somewhat short of desirable. In the evenings the students piled into my apartment to study. But that was not ideal either, so I set out to remedy the situation.

I sought assistance from the particular missionary responsible for such matters. He informed me that it was another missionary's duty. Next I approached the newly designated man with my dilemma. That man briskly stated that he would have nothing to do with the situation, because it was not his responsibility. Again I started down the what-appeared-to-be-appropriate chain of command for domestic affairs and wound up with the same answers. Not wanting to start another compound disagreement, with war nerves so tense, and yet not being willing to drop the matter, I was frustrated. Furthermore, electrical wiring extended far beyond my nonexistent mechanical talents.

Finally I decided to try the military for my electrical help. Yes, indeed, they would come and wire the Saigon Adventist Hospital School of Nursing. Separately I notified the two missionaries whom I'd previously approached and told them of my success with the military engineering department. Both appeared pleased. Neither man objected.

The following Sunday an engineer complete with his squad of GI helpers pulled up to the mission in an army jeep. The men worked proficiently. By early afternoon the necessary wires dangled from the ceilings and electrical outlet boxes manned the walls. My servant and I attempted to appease their voracious appetites and show appreciation for their work by preparing dinner.

Evidently the dinner did not satisfy the gray-haired engineer. A few days later he appeared at my door demanding pay for the previous Sunday's work. As gently as possible I informed him that he could talk to the business manager regarding the matter. Quickly he told me money did not happen to be the type of remuneration he had in mind at the moment. His breath reeked with alcohol. Chills of fright overtook me as he staggered toward me. Silently I asked Heaven for guidance: "Help, Lord. What do I do now?"

Taking a big deep breath in an attempt to sound calm, I answered, "Mister, you don't understand. I'm a missionary. I came out here to help the Vietnamese." We argued for several minutes, but he kept his distance. Suddenly, abruptly, he turned around and stormed out of my apartment, shouting, "You still owe me something anyway. Someday I'll get my pay." He never did, let me assure you.

The nursing students came mostly from Buddhist environments. Only a small percentage claimed Christianity, so the school became a missionary endeavor. The curriculum included Bible classes taught by the Vietnamese pastors, but I hoped we could love the students into Christianity rather than have them feel obligated or forced into the church because of professional pressures, a situation which sometimes occurs in the mission field. Every evening someone had worship with them—the responsibility passing among the missionaries and Vietnamese pastors. One of the doctors played the accordion with brilliance, and he taught the girls multitudes of gospel songs and choruses which they loved to sing. His worships were the students' favorites, I'm sure. We used a little folding pump organ for the services when the accordion was not available, but it lacked that certain enthusiastic splendor. Besides, I made so many strange-sounding mistakes on it that the students burst out laughing, with me joining them. Now I wished that climbing trees had not been such a temptation during my piano-lesson days.

As time passed, some of the girls found the love of God. A number requested church membership. The mission family thrilled with each baptism. On one occasion eight students were baptized, and we nearly all jumped with sheer joy. At the end of my term, the school comprised forty students and twenty of them had joined the church. Sometimes, however, I feel we place too much emphasis on the number of baptisms rather than on the quality of changed lives.

Also I found excitement in the tender nursing care most of the students gave their patients, care which offered such a contrast to the calloused indifference demonstrated by others not exposed to the "loving" aspects of Christianity. I constantly prayed that God would conceal from the sensitive students the difficulties the missionaries had among themselves. While I do not know if they were aware of them, the girls seemed to forgive us. Perhaps they understood that we frail foreigners did not tolerate problems such as war as patiently as they.

In my fond eyes, the nursing students' beauty lay unsurpassed. Their delicate features and perfect complexions at times stirred up envy within me. Long black hair swung to their dainty waists, and their slim figures made us foreigners feel like oxen in comparison. During the week the students donned their pink hospital uniforms and, after work, blouses and pantaloons that resembled pajamas. But on Sabbaths and special occasions they wore the traditional Vietnamese dress, the *ao dais*. It consisted of a close-fitting bodice with a long tunic slit up the sides and worn with white or black pantaloons. I acquired several *ao dais* myself, and the girls eagerly demonstrated the proper Vietnamese feminine manners that should accompany the dress.

Probably I allowed myself to become closer to the nursing students than a true administrator should. After all, I was scarcely a year older than some of them, which presented problems in a culture that highly respects white hair. Furthermore, my basic personality just does not naturally bend toward sternness. Discipline was hard for me. I readily admit to my frequent exhibitions of immaturity in judgment. But I learned some important lessons in consistency and life in general, thanks to my fellow missionaries and wise Vietnamese co-workers.

Somehow the girls must have known that I loved them in spite of my mistakes in dealing with them, because they flooded me with their affection. They called me Young Mother and constantly sought my advice on their romantic affairs. After I left, I received a letter from one of the students, who said, "Some student get new boyfriend, but I still use old one." Once as I prepared to fly home for a vacation, twenty-seven girls invaded my apartment to "assist" me in my packing; then they all stood at the mission gate to welcome me when I returned. On one occasion they gave me a huge lei which they had made for me. And when I passed by, they embarrassed me by shouting out in unison, "Beautiful, beautiful." I remember the time the students and I played football for PE, and I stepped on the dainty foot of one of my girls and broke her little toe. Even she forgave me. They took care to celebrate my birthday in their own special way, though they brought me little gifts all year long. I'm the world's greatest cat lover, and my students saw to it that my supply of felines never ceased. How I loved those nursing students!

Frequently on Saturday nights we had parties together. One Christmas the nursing students from Southwestern Union College sent my girls huge boxes of gifts. The Kate Lindsay Hall residents of Loma Linda University supplied the dormitory with matching bedspreads. Such expressions of thoughtfulness thrilled the girls.

Sometimes at night after study hour, they scrambled up the stairs, swarmed into my apartment, and demurely asked, "Would you please come kiss us all good night, Co* Bennett?" Giving good-night kisses to fifty girls can be time consuming, believe me.

Some nights they insisted that I join them in their dormitory, especially when the fighting came close. We had an unspoken understanding between us that should our end come, we all wanted to go together. During such night sessions the girls seemed most responsive to my religious philosophy. I explained why we need never fear, because a living God exists who loves us each one dearly.

One evening the fighting seemed terribly close. In fact, the tut-tut-tut of machine-gun fire sounded as if it were almost outside the gate. The terrified students flocked around me. Then suddenly their frightened expressions changed as they said, "Co Bennett, we will not be afraid if you aren't." I didn't deserve their confidence, but God provided strength.

Unfortunately, I never had the time to learn Vietnamese well enough to converse freely. It is such a difficult language that I just couldn't pick it up on my own. Although I took some lessons from a tutor, I was so exhausted during the time he could fit into my schedule that I would always fall asleep. At first the students understood almost no English. We included

---

*Vietnamese for "Miss."

intensive English courses in the curriculum so that after graduation they would have access to the medical publications printed in English and still continue learning if they chose to. Otherwise, because little scientific material is translated into Vietnamese, the level of knowledge they attained at graduation would be final. But until their English comprehension increased to a sufficient level, Vietnamese nurses from the hospital translated all the nursing lectures.

Every morning the students and I walked the mile from the compound to the hospital. Curfew supposedly existed till seven in the morning, but at six thirty no guards bothered us—usually. On the way to the hospital we passed a Vietnamese army base. One morning they must have had new troops—soldiers who didn't know us—manning the machine guns at its gate.

As we entered the main street from the alley, we looked directly at the barrels of several mounted guns aimed at us. Floodlights glared into our eyes. Waves of cold fear raced up and down my spine. Suddenly I found presence of mind to start waving my nurse's cap frantically. The students followed my example. Immediately the lights went off and the guns turned to their resting position. Gratefully the students and I literally galloped on to the hospital.

Ordinarily I enjoyed the leisurely walk to the hospital in the coolness of the morning shadows. Saigon was just waking up for the day. Sometimes GI's slipped out of the little shacks, buttoning up their green shirts and waving good-bye to the small Oriental women standing in the doorways. As I passed by, the aroma of rice cooking drifted through the open windows and doors. I caught glimpses of little children and adults squatting on their heels, efficiently stuffing piles of rice into their mouths with long wooden chopsticks. Oriental chants floated through the crisp air from multitudes of radios.

One day I was briskly striding toward the hospital when suddenly the blaring air horns of an approaching convoy startled me. Above their shrillness came what sounded like a thousand shouts intermingled with continuous wolf whistles.

"What on earth is going on?" I wondered. Glancing sideways into the street, I suddenly realized that all the commotion was for my benefit. Truck after truck packed with GI's rushed by me, the fellows vigorously waving their arms and caps at me, their faces beaming with smiles. In return I waved my nurse's cap at them. The sight of an American civilian woman on the Saigon streets wasn't too common after the 1968 Tet offensives. I later heard of another time when a GI friend from my hometown rode on one of the passing convoys. Recognizing me, he shouted and shouted at me, but I did not see him or hear his voice because of all the noise.

The walk to the hospital was the only leisure time of my day. The mornings passed rapidly since I supervised the students' patient care and conducted ward conferences for them. But I tried to help as much as possible in their work. When the Communists played havoc with Saigon's water-supply lines, helping sometimes included carrying heavy pails of water up three flights of stairs from the hospital well so that patients could still get their daily baths and have drinking water. Usually we used the piped-in city water to save the precious well water only for emergencies.

Working with the students at the hospital always proved interesting. They expected me, their teacher, to be the fountain of all wisdom. The fact was that my one year out of school just hadn't bestowed all knowledge upon me. The first morning I accompanied them to the hospital, the students grabbed me and literally pulled me into a patient's room. In terror they whispered, "What we do now?"

A thin man lay on a stretcher sandwiched on the floor in between the other wooden beds in the small room. His body shook and twisted in contortions with each gasping breath. I felt completely helpless. In my own panic I couldn't think of anything to do except hold his hand gently with my hands to keep him from injuring himself. His diagnosis was tetanus, a fairly common disease in Vietnam but something I knew practically nothing about then. But I learned.

Many times when I couldn't come up with answers either to my students' or my own medical questions, I would dash downstairs to the doctors' offices and pester them for answers. Their patience deserved a medal. One doctor affectionately called me "Chicken Little." When my head popped in his office door, he'd smile broadly and teasingly chirp, "What does Chicken Little need to know now?"

The patients of Vietnam suffered from the same gamut of illnesses that befall human beings anywhere, including cancer, gallbladder attacks, heart problems, stomach ulcers, arthritis, and tuberculosis, to mention a few. Then of course the multitude of health problems that plague all underdeveloped nations loomed large, and the war seemed to intensify them. Our hospital served only the civilian population. Other medical help was available for both the Vietnamese and American military casualties.

When heavy fighting surrounded Saigon, or if the city received frequent rocket attacks, the hospital doubled its already heroic efforts to accommodate the injured. One of the doctors had a jar filled with all the bullets and shrapnel that he had removed from patients.

The students and I learned together during such times. I well remember teaching the students how to dress the chasm where a woman's shoulder had once been—the result of a Communist rocket when it zoomed into her house. I had never seen anything even resembling such a wound before. Gingerly I showed the students what to do. Then there were the torsos riddled with hosts of tiny black holes from claymore mine explosions. We had to delicately care for them along with the gruesome stumps of amputated limbs. Daily we viewed sickening wounds from bullets and bombs.

I hate war. The injuries we treated every day seemed so unnecessary. It was all I could do to keep from weeping as the students and I cared for the patients. I will never forget the haunting, emaciated looks of anguish on their faces.
Sometimes I slipped upstairs to the roof where I could weep in solitude when the continuous exposure to suffering became too much for me. At times I found my students doing the same thing. Then we wept together. We also discovered the patients' relatives up there sobbing. All I could do was put my arms around them. I wouldn't be surprised if the palm in front of the hospital didn't grow an extra inch from the moisture of the tears shed down on it from the rooftop.

Even though the medical staff worked valiantly, not all the patients lived. When someone died, we wrapped the body in a sheet. Since the morgue sat in the middle of the hospital courtyard, we had to carry it down the winding staircase in full view of the sometimes frightened visitors, relatives, and waiting outpatients.

Death is particularly frightening in lands where spirit worship prevails. The family would then light candles over the body in the little morgue until the black intricately carved funeral wagon arrived. But one day I watched a tiny woman struggle to pick up a wrapped body much larger than herself and seat herself in a cyclo with the body stretched across her lap. I then saw the cyclo spurt out into the street and become trapped in the perennial traffic jam, with the white form clearly visible, jutting up above her. (I was on the third floor and could not leave the students at that moment to help her.) She probably did not have enough money to have a funeral for her loved one; I suppose she buried him herself. That scene haunted me.

Why did life have to be so ugly at times? Was there absolutely nothing I could do to relieve their pain? Couldn't the church do something to get the message of Christ to Vietnam faster; to let them know that a better day was coming; that they could see their deceased loved ones someday? Was there nothing I could do to let them know that I really cared? The questions endlessly churned within me.

The sadness I encountered during my two-year stay in Vietnam I shall never forget. The throngs of sick babies and children were heartrending. The pediatric department of our hospital constantly overflowed. Many times the parents did not bring the children for medical help until they lay dying. By then it was too late for us to do anything, but the parents couldn't always understand.

On one occasion a Vietnamese soldier brought his sick child to the hospital. We did everything possible to save him, but he died shortly after his admission. The father then became so furious with us that he picked up a wooden stool and started beating the closest male nurse over the head. I stood in a corner of the room watching the episode. While I wanted to rescue the nurse, fright kept my feet glued to the floor. The poor father was mad with grief. The nurse survived the ordeal without injury, however.

On another occasion, a young mother brought her three-year-old son to our hospital. But again it was too late, and the child died on one of the stretchers on the floor—we didn't even have time to transfer him to a bed upstairs. The woman's whole body shook with sobs that echoed throughout the building. Placing my arms around her in my puny attempts to give comfort, I noticed the terrible pain of bereavement that filled her flawless face. She was a beautiful Oriental woman. I glanced down at the still form of her son. His light skin and fair hair told me instantly that his father was an American, but her perfect features reproduced themselves on his tiny face. Then between sobs she told me how deeply she had loved the child's father during the year he had been stationed at Ton Son

Nhut. But he had a wife and children in the United States, and he didn't even know that he had fathered a son in Vietnam. Her family had disowned her for producing a part-Caucasian child, because her father had great wealth. Now the last of anything having value or meaning in her life was gone. I, too, stood there grief stricken in empathy, but I could find no words to say.

Of course what made our work rewarding were the many recoveries we saw in our patients. Our hospital produced miracles, considering the equipment and supplies available to us. Daily, patients walked down those circular stairs singing our praises. (We certainly did not carry them all down to the morgue.)

Motorcycle accidents were so common that we had our own abbreviation to use in diagnosis—HBH, which meant "hit by Honda." I was always amazed that more people weren't injured when I saw the cycles weave in between gigantic military trucks with such daring abandon.

One day we admitted a teen-ager with the HBH diagnosis. His condition was serious in that he had sustained a severe head injury. We observed him carefully for a few hours. The doctors always hesitated to do neurosurgery since they were not trained in it. Besides, the hospital had no equipment or trained nursing personnel to handle the problem either. In fact, no facilities existed in the whole country for neurosurgery except at the American military hospitals, and battle casualties filled them. As the hours passed, his unconsciousness deepened. The hospital staff prayed. Then, little by little, consciousness returned, and that boy walked down the winding staircase by himself a few days later. The lad's Buddhist father came back several times to tell us that now he knew for sure there was a living God. I do not know if either he or the boy embraced Christianity later, but the healing was a definite miracle, and the news spread everywhere.

Another time the hospital completely exhausted its supply

of IV fluids except for a few bottles of a seldom-used
preparation of glucose and alcohol that we had accumulated
from somewhere—probably from the U.S. military hospital
down the street after they cleaned their shelves. Rather than
let the really sick patients dehydrate further, the doctors
ordered the strange alcohol infusion until we could find fresh
supplies of fluids. Finding them happened to be no small
problem in war-torn Saigon. The military hospitals could not
always spare their supplies. The angels must have been busy
turning the "wine" back into water, because no ill effects
transpired. Just as the last bottles of alcohol solution dripped
into the veins of the patients, our medical director received a
telegram stating that a full supply of IV fluids would fly in
immediately by air-force transport from Hawaii. The medical
staff nearly danced for joy. God never let us down.

So the hospital consumed my mornings. Classroom
teaching filled the afternoons. That left my evenings free for
lecture preparation and the multitude of details that
administrators must attend to, such as developing courses,
scheduling, constructing curricula, attempting to develop the
pretense of a library system with the books that we solicited,
besides the secretarial work, and more student supervision
during evening and night shifts. Workdays frequently stretched
into eighteen-to-twenty-hour ordeals week after week. On one
occasion I worked for nine months straight without a day off.
Then during the precious sleeping hours, the ever-present war
noises made rest difficult.

Sometimes fatigue gripped me with such force that I felt my
body might collapse almost any minute. Yet, in spite of the
work load, I actually stayed away from my duties because of
illness only one day—a minute bout of dysentery. I thank God
for the way He strengthened me. The mission just did not have
enough help for the enormous work loads that the Saigon
situation demanded. The other missionaries suffered the

same plight. I certainly was not alone on the frustrating
merry-go-round of too much work, not enough hours, no
energy. However, I felt that some of my co-workers exhibited a
maturity that I had not yet developed, that it stabilized them in
their ability to tolerate the overloads. Occasionally we found a
few hours here and there for play.

Sometimes I envisioned my classmates' Stateside
forty-hour workweeks with much jealousy. I longed at times to
abandon responsibility and have time for play—and sometimes
I did!

Of course, not all mission assignments are so grueling.
Church officials told us that Saigon was just about the most
difficult place in the world for which to find missionaries at that
time. Now I don't know if it actually was so, or if the men were
merely trying to make us feel courageous. That is not for me to
dispute. But our union president sometimes suggested that
when we Saigon missionaries went to heaven, God would see
to it that we received mansions "right on the golf course."

More School Bells

Faculty meetings, over which I had to preside, were the bane of my existence. As time passed, we had a total of forty-five students in three classes running simultaneously. To accommodate the added load, our faculty leaped up to twenty part-time teachers and me—the only full-time person. It was hardly what one calls ideal from an administrative angle, but in Saigon, reality took precedence over idealism. I didn't want to take so many students or have so many classes going, but there's a story only my guardian angel fully understands.

A majority of the teachers were old enough to be my parents. Many of them had never taught before and didn't claim to know anything about educational methods. So I supplied the outlines, constructed short teaching guides, and gave them whatever limited advice I could muster up.

My faculty included almost every member of the mission family plus some of the Vietnamese national employees. Then I solicited additional teaching help from GI's stationed in Saigon, American civilians working for the USAID program, and wives whose husbands worked for construction companies under military contracts. They suddenly discovered themselves teaching nutrition, English, anatomy, psychology, sociology, chemistry, physics, physical education, plus every other subject in a typical nursing curriculum. Those teachers—

though they may not have claimed the title—will never know how I appreciated their willingness to contribute to my survival, because the subjects for which no one else appeared, I attempted to handle.

But bringing together people of varying ages, professional backgrounds, nationalities, religions, and personalities to discuss school policies and problems while I tried to lead in a parliamentary way is one of those chapters in my life over which I have completely drawn a thick black curtain. Needless to say, I survived, the teachers taught, and the students learned. How? Only God knows for sure.

At times feelings of inadequacy nearly crushed me. But at my lowest moments some little bit of encouragement would always trickle in—just enough to bolster my confidence and keep me producing. My parents constantly reminded me that "maturity is the ability to tolerate conflict," but their message didn't always register within me.

My parents' letters and tapes cheered me immeasurably. Once my "bolstering" took the form of a surprise letter from my union president in Singapore telling me how proud he was of my demonstration of unusual maturity and stability in dealing with the difficulties of Saigon in 1968. I still have that letter tucked away with my treasures.

Another time a USAID administrator, who taught English for me, made a special trip to my apartment one Sunday afternoon to inform me that I was showing definite administrative talent and that I should pursue it further as a career. He possessed a serious personality and wasn't the type to joke often, but I burst out laughing, thinking he was teasing me. But he informed me that he wasn't joking—that he had come to discuss my future professional life and offer suggestions and directions. Women's liberation and high career development have never been one of my burdens, but at that time—because of the problems I faced—I couldn't even faintly imagine how a woman would voluntarily choose a professional career if staying home were a viable option. At that point I would have been delighted to become a nurse's aide or cleaning lady the rest of my life—just deliver me from management! The most enjoyable moments for me in Saigon were my turns at being hostess and helping to cook for and entertain the multitude of guests that flocked through our compound.

One time I found myself a member of the year-end Union Committee meetings in Singapore. On that occasion it was my responsibility to address the entire committee on some aspect of nursing education and convince it to vote a certain way. Not only did I face a roomful of people, most of whom were old enough to be my parents, but I was just about the only woman present. I absolutely shook with fright, but they must not have known it, because they voted unanimously in favor of my presentation. Maybe they did it from pity, but that committee usually wasn't that emotional.

Only God fully understood the true reticence of my personality for assuming leadership and how low my tolerance for frustration and conflict was at that time. I know our heavenly Father certainly was near. He gave me courage and strength to buckle down and stick with the job even though I hated it at times. The struggling school and its terribly green administrator managed to endure the waves of discouraging setbacks that always wash the shores of any endeavor.

Scheduling forty-plus students through a thirty-bed hospital was not always practical. Besides, future nurses needed a larger exposure to the gamut of medical problems indigenous to Vietnam than was available in our small hospital. The school's road to accreditation by the Vietnamese government lay in affiliation with the local hospitals, so the authorities told us.

Therefore, I set out to acquire affiliation privileges from various medical institutions in the area. Finally, arrangements with seven Saigon government hospitals evolved after months of hassle and red tape with the Vietnamese Health Department. Then came the myriad of details and Oriental protocol involved with the administrators of each of the hospitals in setting up schedules.

The most enjoyable parts of the whole operation were the open cyclo rides to and from the hospitals—when I could persuade the translator not to take a taxi or the truck. Regardless of our method of transportation, we'd invariably get stuck in some traffic jam, hemmed in by convoys, jeeps, motorcycles, and anything else imaginable. It gave me an opportunity to collect my thoughts and calm myself. Waves of sheer terror rushed through me as I talked with Vietnamese officials and administrators. I could almost feel my knees shaking and teeth chattering as we'd walk up to the steps of the administrative offices. My translator knew how I felt, so as she interpreted, she extended the ideas so that I could collect my thoughts between speeches.

The translator, a dainty Vietnamese woman, was one of the wisest, most organized individuals I've ever known. She juggled the roles of wife, mother, teacher, nurse, dietitian, and assistant director of nursing service into her twenty-four-hour day with such efficiency that it often made me envious.

The affiliations with the Vietnamese government hospitals turned out to be a unique experience. At least the students learned great respect for our Adventist hospital, inadequate as it was.

The other hospitals offered little individual patient care, leaving such measures up to the relatives of the sick. If none came, the patients simply lay quietly in their discomfort, unattended in many cases.

I know of one instance in another hospital where a baby died because the mother herself was too ill to go to the hospital to tend the infant, and other relatives lived too far away to accommodate. In our mission hospital we gave total patient care regardless of the presence or absence of relatives—in many cases we wished the relatives would stay home since they sometimes interfered with our program—like feeding unconscious patients, for example. If the mother had brought her young child to our hospital, we might possibly have been able to treat the infant.

One time a certain cancer patient lay unbathed for three months in one hospital in which the students affiliated. The woman's relatives lived in central Vietnam, but they feared her condition, and no one would come to care for her. She had a protruding brain lesion that continuously oozed a foul-smelling liquid all over her bed. The memories of that odor linger with me to this day. Waves of nausea passed over both the students and me, but the girls continued in the unpleasant task of cleaning her. Such a contented look emanated from her emaciated face when we finally had her comfortable. They changed the sheets only once a week, if they could find fresh supplies that often. Since we couldn't obtain fresh linen, the students took the sheet, washed it out, and placed clean newsprint over the soiled mattress until the sheet dried.

The stench of that particular hospital was so strong that at first I let the students wear masks in an attempt to avert our ever-eminent nausea. Then we washed the floors, using mops and strong disinfectant solution we brought with us.

We had to provide the supplies for the general cleaning and patient care that our students did at the government hospitals each day. The government hospitals just did not have such equipment. Every morning the hospital truck left the compound loaded with students holding in their laps piles of army-donated green towels, basins, soap, powder, mouthwash, and cleaning rags. I refused to let them tend the ill in the midst of unnecessary filth. Lack of sophisticated or even necessary equipment is one thing, but water and soap were usually

available, and I saw no reason for such uncleanliness. We
included permission to clean in the affiliation "contracts." I
must not be unduly harsh toward other hospitals. They usually
did the best they could with the available help. One hospital
hired only one nurse at night for four hundred patients. A
poverty-stricken government involved in a costly war struggled
to operate the hospitals, and inflation was rampant. Naturally
the war effort took priority above civilian medical care.

Part of the students' pediatric experience took place at a
500-bed children's hospital. The students' routine here
included cleaning the wards assigned them as well as patient
care—an old-fashioned concept in nursing today. But how
could I be complacent while watching sick toddlers crawling on
a floor among little piles of human feces surrounded by swarms
of flies, or when mice scampered periodically under the beds?
Older children or parents sat on the same floor, nonchalantly
eating bowls of rice. Outside the hospital lay huge piles of
rotting garbage with rats the size of full-grown cats gnawing
and burrowing quite unconcernedly. But the garbage, the rats,
and the mice happened to be completely beyond my control.

In some respects our overcrowded Adventist hospital
seemed spacious in comparison to the other hospitals. We
usually kept one patient to a bed and packed our hospital with
beds, stretchers, and cots. But the government institutions kept
the number of beds to a minimum and piled the patients into
them. Sometimes five babies lay in one crib. As many as three
adults occupied some "regular" beds. They managed that feat
by placing two patients side by side, then the third person
curled up at the foot and nestled himself halfway between the
other two. I saw three patients to a bed most frequently in
orthopedic wards. If someone had a leg in traction, the second
individual again lay beside him, and the third patient then
crouched his head under the elevated limb, shoving his legs
and feet in between the first two. That third person invariably

lay in a continuous semifetal position. After tonsillectomies,
four children shared the same bed—two at the head and two at
the foot. Vietnamese are small people to begin with, but I never
understood how an ill person tolerated such uncomfortable
positions day in and day out. My heart grieved for them.

In spite of their inadequacies, the affiliations were
beneficial. Both the patients and staff at the government
hospitals loved the girls. Expressions of gratitude actually
emanated from the faces of the patients. Vietnamese doctors
and medical students explained various disease processes and
procedures to the students. The doctors told me how our
students amazed them with the amount of knowledge they
possessed. "They know more than the medical students," I
heard them say several times.

One morning a Vietnamese doctor came to me, his brown
eyes glowing and his English broken, but I understood what he
was trying to say. "Your student very good. I hear your mission
hospital very good. I hear your doctor pray much—alway pray
before operation. I think is very good. I no Christian, but I want
pray."

So the affiliations had evangelistic aspects as well, though I
did not necessarily stress that part. One day I observed one of
my Buddhist students telling her Buddhist patient about the
living God. Then she prayed with her. On Christmas day the
Buddhist students sang Christian carols to Buddhist patients at
one of their affiliation hospitals—it was the students' idea.

Another interesting place the students worked was the
intensive-care unit of a Vietnamese military hospital. During
that time, American helicopters flew in hundreds of wounded
Vietnamese soldiers from the Cambodian front. Through the
windows of the intensive-care unit, I watched the choppers,
filled with litters of wounded men, landing one after another.
"They died like flies" is such a trite, undignified way to express
the end of human life, yet words just cannot express the horror

of what I witnessed in the adjacent emergency area. I had
never seen fresh casualties before. They defied description:
arms and legs ripped off or dangling by jagged pieces of flesh,
blood spurting from gaping holes in the abdomen as orderlies
and nurses wrapped the first-aid bandages, open holes where
eyes once existed. Bullets, it seems, were designed to produce
as much damage to human flesh as possible. Hating war, I
thought of what Harry Emerson Fosdick once wrote: "War's
tragedy is that it uses man's best—his skill, his courage, his
self-sacrifice—to do man's worst."

Some of the casualties the attendants left on the stretchers
to die. The salvageable bodies they whisked off to surgery.
Afterward the wounded soldiers returned to the IC unit with
long incisions covered by thick white bandages.

The men received the best treatment I'd witnessed in
Vietnam outside of our own mission hospital and the U.S.
military hospitals. The tile floor sparkled. Daily baths and
dressing changes comprised part of the routine. Yet the
wounded soldiers never received any medication for pain, no
matter how extensive their wounds. I watched the men writhing
in sheer agony. My heart absolutely ached for them. Some
seemed so young. I learned that the Vietnamese military doctor
in charge of surgery refused to order narcotics for the soldiers
for fear they might become addicted. Although I pleaded with
the physicians to try to relieve their pain, my requests went
unheeded. It seemed extremely unfair.

The nursing students managed their work efficiently, and
we all learned from the military doctors, who supervised the
unit.

Viet Cong captives swelled the patient roster as well. At first
I wondered how the students might react at having to care for
their enemy—members of the force that killed their fathers and
brothers and whose rockets devastated their homes. But I
observed no difference in the treatment they gave their own

men and the VC prisoners. The dressing changes, baths, mouth care, and back care they rendered with equal tenderness to all patients.

Heavy chains encircled the wrists and ankles of the prisoners, fastening them to their beds, not that they could have escaped with those wounds if they had wanted to. The metal bonds scraped the skin, leaving it raw. I found the students wrapping gauze around the irritated areas so that the chains would be more comfortable. Weak smiles of appreciation rose from the prisoners' lips.

One day, near the end of the affiliation at the military intensive-care unit, I discovered a student weeping just outside the door. Immediately I investigated, and in between her sobs she told me how one of the patients looked so much like her own soldier-boyfriend. "I see patient who look like my boyfriend. I no hear from my boyfriend for long time. I think he in Cambodia to fight like patient who here. My brother killed in DMZ last year. I see patient look like he too. I very sad." The tears continued to flow. I embraced her, but what could I say? My brother and boyfriend lived in the safety of peaceful lands.

I decided the students also needed exposure to the sophisticated equipment and excellent care given to the American soldiers in the U.S. military hospitals. It would be a tremendous contrast to either our mission hospital or the Vietnamese government hospitals. How all by myself I ever amassed the courage to approach the commander of the Third Field Hospital, the chief army nurse for the entire military in Vietnam, and finally the Surgeon General's office to get affiliation privileges remains a miraculous mystery to me. How I longed for my translator to hide behind when confronting the American brass—not that her tiny figure covered much of *me*. But now I had to do all my own talking. If what I said didn't make sense, I had no appropriate pauses with which to conjure more tangible ideas.

But the military officials possessed compassion, I
discovered. On one occasion they invited me to be their guest
of honor at a dinner at the officers' dining room. There they told
me how proud they were of me—"a little American
girl"—having the courage to start a nursing school in the midst
of the Vietnam war. If they had only known my real feelings,
they may not have been so impressed. Words cannot explain
the sheer joy bubbling in my heart the first time my Vietnamese
student nurses walked past the American guard into the
spotless Third Field Army Hospital. It was beyond my wildest
imagination that someday my church would operate it and my
students would serve in it.

God certainly blessed the nursing school. Strangely
enough, it received a certain amount of inadvertent acclaim.
One hundred fifty applications swamped our desks for the
fifteen available places in the second class, and around three
hundred for the third class. Vietnamese government officials
and high-ranking military brass told the missionaries it was the
best school in Vietnam. An American marine general stationed
near the DMZ flew down to visit once, and other important
people such as President Nixon's Undersecretary of State
stopped by. Ministers from the Adventist union and division
headquarters in Singapore reported that it was an outstanding
feature of our church program in Vietnam. Eventually the
nursing school received full accreditation with the Vietnamese
government, something people told us over and over again
would never happen. Naturally such bits of news cheered me,
but I knew the results were not due merely to human
efforts—God blessed us beyond our highest expectations.

My First
Helicopter Ride

"Hey, Chicken Little! Have to go out to the orphanage right now. Want to go? We should be back fairly soon. If you want to go, let's beat it."

The man held his stocky frame erect. His hair, lightly shaded with gray, lay neatly combed, yet two strands fell disobediently down his forehead, almost touching those kind blue eyes that often twinkled with mischief as they did now. His brawny hands cupped around his mouth as he shouted up to me.

My four-room apartment lay directly on top of his in the old yellow mission house. Whenever it was necessary to relay some message to me, he or his wife rang a bell on their back porch, and I'd run out to my balcony so that we could communicate further. Occasionally my running to the balcony in response to the ting-a-ling made me feel a bit like Pavlov's dog salivating in response to the bell. And sometimes my salivary glands did start secreting, since both the wife and her servant were culinary artists, and my downstairs neighbors often invited me to share their repasts. Sometimes the bell signaled the arrival of letters from home, which they'd tape to the end of a long stick and hand up to me as I'd bend down way over the railing. And once in a while the gentle tolling indicated momentary doom when my elderly, partially deaf servant forgot that she had left the water running into the bathtub where she washed my clothes. It splashed over the tub top, spilled onto the floor, and ran down into my fellow missionary's kitchen directly below through cracks in my cement floor.

Although it was still early, the humidity of the tropical morning hung heavy, drenching me with a temporary listlessness that only a surprise jaunt could enliven. I am the kind of person who is always ready to go adventuring off somewhere.

"Yeah, sure I want to go. Will be right there," I called down.

In answer, the man placed his feet to a sharp forty-five-degree angle, heels touching each other. Giving me a crisp salute and grinning broadly, he replied, "OK, Chicken Little." My friend had once been an army sergeant, and a faint touch of military still escaped in his mannerisms.

A few minutes later the two missionaries and I found ourselves tucked into the blue Chevy Nova, rolling along the road to the orphanage, a large Buddhist institution housing around two thousand children and located about forty miles outside the city. Its leader had asked our hospital to immunize the children. Then the administrator requested our church to send people out to tell the children stories, and it became the world's largest branch Sabbath School. Ordinarily the group went to the orphanage on Sabbath afternoon, but the administrator had sent a special message begging for someone from the mission to come out that particular morning to a special ceremony.

High-ranking military officers would attend as well as Madam Thieu, the president's wife. The orphanage director was so grateful for what our hospital and church were doing for the children that he wanted us as guests at the ceremony for Madam Thieu's visit. It would also formally open the orphanage since it had not existed long.

We sat in the guests' seats along with U.S. military officers and Vietnamese government officials. After several speeches, a trumpet's blaring, and a flag raising, the short program ended. Though the ceremony was not intended to be religious, I was constantly reminded of Jesus and His love for the children. A sacred air seemed to surround the area.

While the missionaries engaged in conversation with some of the other guests, I started wandering around the premises, watching the children in their saffron robes. One couldn't tell the boys from the girls because all their heads were shaved bare. They politely bowed as I passed. The orphanage consisted of several long separate buildings with reed and mud walls and thatched roofs.

Soon I discovered a helicopter sitting beside one of the thatched huts. Gingerly I walked up and curiously peered in at all the dials and levers in the cockpit. I stood on tiptoe to get a better view. It was, I decided, the closest I'd probably ever come to a helicopter, and I was excited since I'm an aviatrix at heart.

Suddenly a tall green-clad figure appeared from the shadows. His deep voice startled me as I stood there intently looking at the machine.

"Whatcha doing, lady?"

"Oh, I'm just looking at your chopper. I've never been this close to one before. Is it OK if I take a peek?"

"Oh, sure, lady, keep right on looking. Sure is good to see a roundeye.* Whatcha doin' in 'Nam?" A quizzical expression crossed his handsome face.

"I'm a Seventh-day Adventist missionary in Saigon," I answered matter-of-factly.

"Wow, a missionary! That's groovy. I wish I could do something to really help these people. All I do is fly around in this dumb bird all day, throwing out propaganda to villages

_____
*An expression GI's used to identify Caucasian women.

saying that they're going to be wiped out if they don't join the government. Or we fly generals around—that's why we're here today. Sometimes I'm assigned to missions where we go blow up and shoot down the enemy. But, good grief . . . they're humans just like we are. I feel rotten some days."

Before I had a chance to answer the GI, my fellow missionaries arrived, ready to depart for Saigon. I waved to the soldier and walked back to the hut where the two men stood waiting for me.

"Wow, I'd sure like to have a chopper ride," I mused to myself.

My mumbled desire was barely audible, but one of the men heard me and snapped, "I've been here three years and haven't had a helicopter ride yet. What makes you think you can get one after you've been here only three months? Besides, they won't take civilian women in helicopters." A you-stupid-little-girl expression covered his thin face as his scornful glare rested on me.

The hot anger of resentment burned inside me. Suddenly indignation covered my bashfulness, and I retorted, "I'm going to ask those guys right now if I can have a ride. Just you wait and see—they'll take me."

"Go on, Chicken Little. Ask them." The older man laughed encouragingly. He seemed rather amused with the conversation between his partner and me.

Valiantly I marched up to the crew who were checking the back rotor. Then I produced the most charming smile I could possibly muster and blurted, "May I have a chopper ride, please?" I listened to my voice as it resounded against the fuselage and echoed back to me. It sounded pathetically naive, its high-pitched tone exposing my nervousness. My heart jumped in spurts within my chest. While I knew they'd consider the little American woman dumb, at that moment I didn't care what they thought.

The answer sounded like the sweetest music to my ears. "Of course you can have a ride! Want to go to Saigon? We've got to drop a general off at Bear Cat, but that won't take long. Sure—climb on." With that the men took my arms and lifted me up into the cabin.

Just then I looked around and saw the missionary running toward the helicopter, his expression of scorn erased. He was smiling now. Quickly he petitioned, "Marilyn, please ask them if I may ride too. The other doctor will drive the car home."

The crew nodded. Suddenly we lifted off. I was strapped in tightly between the general and my fellow missionary. About ten minutes later we landed at Bear Cat, where the general disembarked.Then the craft headed toward Saigon. Suddenly, there in the middle of the air, my co-worker and I turned and faced each other, smiled, and then broke out laughing. We quickly gave one another a silent nod of forgiveness for our childishness a few minutes before. We were friends again.

The helicopter pilot landed the craft right on the mission compound, which had never happened before. As the chopper hovered above the compound grass, all the Vietnamese children darted out of the school building, and adults poured from a meeting in the third-floor church room. Everyone started shouting, "Co Bennett, Co Bennett."

I felt like a celebrity, eliciting so much attention. But my feeling immediately turned to chagrin as I realized that I'd instantly disrupted the whole compound routine. The chopper stood completely surrounded by both brown and white faces. No one else had ever been that close to a helicopter either, so a certain excitement enveloped everyone.

Thanking the pilots as profusely as possible, I jumped to the ground from the cabin. I stood along with the rest of the crowd as the chopper roared skyward. We waved until it flew out of sight. After that, I had greater tolerance for the continuous overhead whir.

Thanksgiving Dinner With the Generals

But now I'm getting just a bit ahead of myself; so let me catch up. Back at the orphanage an American general's social aide invited me to be one of the general's guests for Thanksgiving dinner the next Thursday. His private helicopter would pick me up at Ton Son Nhut and fly me back after the dinner.

It was just too exciting an adventure to turn down, but I knew that I'd better get permission before accepting the invitation. Immediately I dashed off to find the head doctor. His warm answer reflected the twinkle in his eyes. "Of course you may. I wouldn't mind coming myself, but guess the general didn't invite me. Besides being fun it will be good PR for the hospital and mission."

I was flattered! Never before in my life had a general invited me to dinner. Of course, I'd never spent a Thanksgiving in Vietnam before either. There were fifteen thousand GI's stationed on the base. I didn't really know quite what to expect.

Thanksgiving morning finally dawned, though I felt positive Thursday would never come. My favorite GI offered to take me out to the heliport. Since it was my big day, he presented me the choice between the pickup or the back of his borrowed motorcycle.

My hair was freshly curled, and for once every hair sat

neatly in place—a most uncommon occurrence for *my* unruly tresses. My best pink polyester dress and pink shoes completed my Thanksgiving outfit. I even wore nylon stockings—something we women almost never donned in Vietnam. There I stood, trying to look as lovely as possible for my fellow countrymen and their general, and my friend offered me a motorcycle ride—something impossible for me to resist. So I carefully tied my prettiest pink chiffon scarf around my curls and gingerly balanced myself sidesaddle on the back seat of the motorcycle, being extra careful not to ruin either my precious nylons or the dress on the protruding exhaust pipes and other paraphernalia that engulf all motorcycles.

Miraculously both hairdo and dress survived the motorcycle trip to the heliport and the short but exciting helicopter journey to the base camp. We flew high above the rice paddies. As the chopper descended, I noticed that it started hovering over an area on the landing-field pavement marked VIP. Parked just beside it waited a jeep with VIP sprawled in big letters across the metal below the windshield. It was the general's private jeep, complete with chauffeur. I had never before received such treatment. The vehicle jerked along the dusty road to the mess hall where the dinner would be served.

Long tables piled high with festive foods stretched the length of the building. A military band played background music while crowds of khaki-clad men swarmed around the tables. I spotted three other American women in the room, but they appeared to be quite older than I. Immediately I found myself surrounded by men. They all started talking at once, and I didn't know what to say. I wished there were a few more women around to share the attention, which was a bit overwhelming to me. But I took a deep breath and tried to answer all their questions. Before long the men knew all about Saigon Adventist Hospital and the work of our mission in Saigon. In turn, I learned a bit more about army life.

Suddenly the building started shaking violently. The vibrations jostled the tables, colliding the steel cutlery with the glassware in gentle waves as the floor rocked beneath. Explosions filled the air. Bursting artillery throbbed in our eardrums. Through the windows I could see sprawling red flames in the gathering dusk.

A few men left the building hurriedly when the battle started, but most continued to eat with the same nonchalance they would have had at a picnic back home. One officer casually leaned over to me and said, "The camp is surrounded by several thousand VC tonight, but it doesn't seem to be anything to worry about at this point." I wasn't frightened, and when all the men seemed unconcerned about the battle, I saw no reason to be distressed either. We all continued to eat and chat as though nothing had happened.

As soon as dinner ended, the soft background music the band had been playing suddenly turned into blaring rock. Quickly the lights dimmed and men pushed the long tables to the side, leaving a large empty space in the middle of the floor. A large army truck filled with Vietnamese women drove up outside the building. As soon as the women entered the door, the men chose partners and started dancing. Instantly they completely packed the floor. Somehow the thought had never entered my naive brain that a dance automatically went along with Thanksgiving dinner. I'd never been to a dance before in my life.

Then the men began asking me to dance. Embarrassed, I at first stammered, "I . . . um . . . don't know how to dance." Suddenly a host of them confidently answered, "Oh, we'll teach you." How could I explain to a huge roomful of American men that I couldn't dance, and furthermore, that I didn't even want to learn? What could I say without hurting them? It appeared they wanted to dance with me more than with the three older American women or the truckload of dainty Vietnamese girls.

Silently I sent a short heaven-bound request: "Help, God! What do I do now? Tell me what to say."

During those few bewildering moments I just couldn't think of any logical reasons why I shouldn't dance. My mind went blank. All I can remember saying was something to the effect that I was a missionary, and my church didn't approve of dancing. Therefore I would rather not. It didn't make much sense, but somehow the men understood.

Suddenly a tall well-built man walked over and asked me to dance. Still embarrassed, I meekly said, "No, thank you." Obviously the man was inebriated. Instantly he scooped me up in his arms, holding me in midair like one would hold a baby, saying something to the effect that if I wouldn't dance with him, then he'd just hold me. It had happened so suddenly, I absolutely didn't know what to do. I was completely mortified and started struggling to free myself. Immediately a whole group of men surrounded us, tartly shouting, "Put the dame down. She doesn't want to dance." I breathed a quick prayer of relief. After that a group of sober, gentlemanly military officers completely encircled me.

Other than the encounter with the inebriate, I must admit that the situation was a temptation to me. Having a quiet outward personality and ordinary looks, I have never been sought after by the majority of the male population. Never in my entire life had so many men in one place clamored for my companionship. I was overwhelmed. Nevertheless, I felt a great sense of responsibility to uphold the standards of my church and try to witness for God in some way.

Since there were not nearly enough women to make it possible for many men to dance at one time, a large group surrounded my chair and just talked. Naturally they wanted to know why a young American woman would willingly come to Vietnam during the middle of the war. I told them more about our church missions program and my reasons for wanting to help in my particular phase of it. The men asked many questions as the evening went on. I don't know if my witness in that dance hall was appropriate or not, but perhaps some of those officers heard something that would later cause them to give extra thought to the important questions in life. I hope so.

The battle continued all evening long, making it impossible for the helicopter to fly me back to Saigon. And so it became necessary for me to spend the night on the base camp. Feeling both frightened and embarrassed, I couldn't decide which to fear the most—the VC parked just outside the camp with their artillery or the amorousness of my drunken fellow countrymen. Needless to say, I was not entirely comfortable. But the men gallantly placed us women in an empty barracks complete with green folding cots, and then they plastered a big sign over the front entrance: Off Limits to All Men.

By then I was so tired, I staggered over to one of the cots close to the door and plopped down. I slipped under the green-and-brown camouflage quilt with a sigh of relief mingled with a grateful prayer of thanks. The cots were placed right at the open door that led to the bunker just a few steps away. From the pounding of the artillery, it was quite probable that we might need to use that bunker after all, the men told us.

As I lay there on that narrow cot, feeling the rumbling vibrations of the explosions around the camp, my mind churned. Over and over I promised myself that I would never again accept a general's invitation if I could just somehow make it back to Saigon in one piece. I envisioned the headlines on the back of the *Review:* "SDA Missionary Nurse Wounded on U.S. Army Base While Spending Evening With 15,000 Troops." Then I giggled to myself, pulled the quilt up over my head in an attempt to cut out the battle roars, and fell asleep.

Early the next morning the Vietnamese sunbeams crept silently into the barracks, finally piercing my eyelids with their brilliance. I remember how thankful I felt as I looked up at the sunlight streaming in, and I silently breathed a prayer of thanks.

Later that morning the helicopter flew me back to Saigon, again landing right on the compound grass. And again the commotion disrupted school and the other activities, but I was grateful to be home.

"Lady, You Would Have Been Killed"

A lot of fighting took place around Saigon following the Tet offensive. It was dangerous to travel farther than just a few miles outside the city. Road mines frequently blew up convoys and civilian traffic. When we did travel outside the city, we often saw fresh evidences of attacks made the day or night before. Destroyed bridges, mutilated bodies, and burned-out vehicles or houses lined the road. Every night we could hear the pounding of the heavy artillery only a few miles out, and from the mission we could see the red and yellow flashes from explosions.

Confinement to the city became depressing. We had no place to go, no way to escape the continual whir of helicopters landing and taking off from Ton Son Nhut. The roaring jets above and the blaring traffic jams just outside the mission gate added to the noisy scene. The buildings of Saigon stand squashed together, and through the ever-open windows came both American rock music and Vietnamese chants from portable radios. The cacophony blasted incessantly through the hot air. Sometimes all I wanted was a tiny bit of space to stretch my arms as far as they would reach without touching anything and to revel in a few minutes of utter silence. Noise, coupled with my rigorous daily routine, exhausted me.

Loving the outdoors, and being a child at heart, I longed to run away from the pandemonium, the crush, and the work load of Saigon to some lazy, quiet stream surrounded by high mountains and just bask in the sheer luxury of physical and mental peace. But war-torn Vietnam offered me no such respite.

At times the green rice paddies skirting the villages outside Saigon summoned me. But military intelligence considered the outlying villages unsafe. The VC supposedly infested them. Even so, the temptation to go skipping along the little brown paths in and around the paddies was great. At times my longing for escape was greater than my fear of danger—or my good judgment.

One Sabbath afternoon the trapped-in feelings engulfed me. My favorite GI must have read my mind, because after dinner he invited me to go for a ride with him on his borrowed motorcycle. Always ready for adventure, I readily accepted, and the black Suzuki roared out the mission gate into the usual confusion on the main street.

We whizzed in and around the buses, trucks, and cyclos with my arms clutched firmly around his waist. Trying to be heard above the traffic din, I shouted, "Hey, let's get out of Saigon and go riding through some of the villages."

"OK. That sounds fine, but how do we get out of these traffic jams into the country?" My friend turned his head just slightly to yell his reply back to me when suddenly a gigantic army truck loomed up directly in front. Spontaneously he gripped the cycle brakes. Catapulting forward and letting out a wild screech in the process, I nearly flew off the seat. "Well, Marilyn, I'm really not deliberately trying to kill you," he yelled a moment later. "But by all means, let's hit the villages. You tell me where."

"There is some neat stuff way out past Ton Son Nhut on the road to Tay Ninh. That's the opposite direction from Long Binh Post, so you'd get to see some new scenery."

"Toward Tay Ninh! There's been a bit of fighting out that way this week, so I hear. I wouldn't want anything to happen to you. But if you're game, I am. But what on earth would I tell the good doctors back at the mission if I don't get you back in one piece?" The deafening roar of the surrounding cyclos nearly drowned out his voice.

"Don't worry. I'm a hardy soul. Nothing is going to happen to either of us," I replied. "Besides, the fighting was more toward the Cambodian border, and that's about seventy miles away. We can't possibly go that far this afternoon. I'm not scared."

As we sped on out past the airbase, the pavement became patchy. We bounced along from chuckhole to chuckhole, laughing and singing Sabbath choruses at the top of our lungs. The vehicle congestion soon thinned out, and we had the road to ourselves as we sped on past miles of luscious green rice paddies. The villages we passed showed evidence of recent battles. Bullet holes sprinkled the walls, and roofs had been partially blown off. However, we couldn't dwell on the negative. It was refreshing just to be out of the city.

The air was clear and quiet. The blue sky seemed to smile down. The only sounds in the far distance were the rumble of the motorcycles and the gentle whirring of the ever-present helicopters. The stillness drenched my soul with a silent peace and inner happiness.

"Hey, let's get off and walk through the paddies for a few minutes. Wouldn't that be fun?" I asked, gently nudging him in the ribs with my elbow. With that he came to a flying halt, and I dug my knees into the seat to keep from landing in the dirt. "Help! Don't kill me yet."

Unfolding his long legs from around the cycle, he stood up straight. "Hang loose, Babe. Nothing is going to happen to you as long as I'm around. Sure is good to stop. My seat was getting sore."

Parking the cycle at the side of the road bordering a spacious rice paddy, we started chasing each other back and forth along the mud paths that penetrated the rice fields, laughing all the time. Then we took our shoes off and went wading. The warm mud squished up through our toes. The carefree spirit of childhood returned. I was happy. A crowd of Vietnamese gathered to watch us—a rather strange sight, no doubt—two Americans racing up and down the rice paddies. But we didn't mind.

Across the expanse of the rice paddies we noticed a thick clump of palm trees. They had something slightly mysterious about them—there seemed to be strange-looking objects underneath. Was it just another village—or could it be something else?

My friend stood looking intently toward the secluded clump of trees. The look of adventure seemed to dance in his eyes. I glanced up at his tall figure again and laughed to myself. His black hair, ruffled from the windy cycle ride, stuck straight up. Big beads of perspiration dotted his forehead. The tail of his blue-and-red plaid shirt hung loosely over his rolled-up navy trousers. Black mud covered his feet.

Somehow he just didn't look like a soldier right then. He wasn't supposed to be out of his military uniform, but that was the furthest thought from his mind at the moment. I knew what thoughts churned within him. Turning to me, he whispered, "Say, let's go over to those palm trees and explore that village, or whatever it is over there." He pointed in the direction of the palms.

Somehow his idea just didn't sound too good. Thinking of just what to say, I didn't answer for a moment. The mud had started to dry on my bare feet, so I rubbed one foot on top of the other in an effort to remove the cakey substance. Then I spoke up forcefully, "No, we must go home. Look, the shadows are starting to get long. We've got to get back to the mission before dark or the missionaries will wonder what happened. It'll take a while to get back into Saigon anyway."

"Yeah, guess you're right." His voice sounded halfhearted and disappointed. He loved the unknown, and the monotony of the military seemed almost unbearable to him at times. Heading back to Saigon and then Long Binh Post was probably the last thing he wanted to do.

We hopped on the motorcycle and sped back to Saigon. Dashing in the gate just before the sun sank behind the buildings, we joined the missionaries for sundown worship. Everyone sang lustily. For some reason I listened closely to the words as we sang: "Safe am I, safe am I, In the hollow of His hand. . . . No ill can harm me. No foe alarm me. . . . He keeps both day and night." My thoughts turned to the afternoon excursion. But soon another song rang out, and my attention shifted to something else.

After worship the GI caught a military truck back to his post, and I walked out to my office to work the rest of the evening. My spirits cheerful once again, I was ready to throw myself into the multitude of waiting tasks. A few hours later, without giving the afternoon excursion a second thought, I closed my office, trudged upstairs to my apartment, and went to bed.

During the night, Communist rockets pounded the city. I was so used to such commotion that I ceased to pay attention to it. Instead I just rolled over in bed and continued to sleep soundly. Early the next morning the sunbeams sprinkled into the bedroom, announcing the arrival of a new day despite the night of violence. My morning ritual included listening to the radio. That Sunday the newscaster surprised me by stating that the VC had landed the night's rocket attack from the same village where the GI friend and I had been romping the previous afternoon. Without a doubt, the crowd that had gathered to watch us had contained VC.

Gratefully I bowed my head and whispered a quick prayer

of thanks. "O God, I don't always deserve Your
protection—You know that. I do not even try to stay safe
sometimes. . . . You're so good to me. But You know me—You
know I can't live all cooped up forever and still get my work
done. You know how I have to get out and go. . . . Honest, I
don't mean to make it hard on You. . . . Forgive me."

Again life took on its routine. Stacks of paper work lay piled
on my office desk. As my weary fingers picked up the pen to
write out more curriculum revisions, I sighed. I sat there
inwardly grumbling about the responsibilities that rested on me
and about my lack of knowledge as to how to handle
administrative details. Suddenly a shadow crossed my desk.
Startled, I looked up to see a tall man standing in the doorway.

"Good morning, Miss Bennett. I'm John Stanley from the
refugee program of USAID. The nurse in charge at the hospital
sent me over to speak to you. Do you think you and some of
your students could come down to the delta and immunize
about five thousand refugees? We would send a helicopter for
you and provide food and lodging, since it might take a couple
of days." The sun danced over the brass buttons on his green
uniform.

"Well, I'll talk it over with the doctors and see what we can
work out. They are interested in this. It sounds like fun. I
personally don't see why we couldn't. When would you want
us?" I questioned. Wiping the perspiration from my brow, I
tilted my head back to look up into his face.

"I've got to verify this with my Vietnamese counterpart, but
what about two weeks from Monday and Tuesday—possibly
Wednesday? I'll let you know for sure by military phone."

"OK. That sounds good. If our doctors approve, we'll get
the stuff ready." I watched the man climb into his waiting jeep
and disappear into the distance.

The doctors did agree to cooperate, we received a
confirming phone call, and we made the necessary

preparations. The students and I waited eagerly for Monday to come. But on Monday, instead of the helicopter's arrival, word came saying that the Vietnamese official in charge of the refugees had changed his mind and did not want them immunized. In the bustle of the busy routine at the hospital, I soon forgot the incident.

However, several days later the USAID official appeared at the mission again. Apologetically he explained how his Vietnamese counterpart had become angry with him over the delegation of authority in some administrative detail and had canceled several programs outlined for the refugees. Then suddenly his tone became very serious. He spoke slowly.

"Miss Bennett, I am not a religious person. But God must have changed the Vietnamese official's mind to keep you from coming. Lady, you'd have been killed. The afternoon you were to have arrived, the VC started an offensive in our area. The first night you would have been there, they invaded our USAID compound. It was terrible! They sneaked up on our barracks and blew it up. The only way we escaped death was by playing dead. You see, the smoke from the explosions clouded the air, and since it was quite dark, we hid under some rubble on the floor. When they found us, they couldn't tell whether we were dead or alive, and, thank God, they took us for dead."

He paused to wipe the sweat from his tanned forehead and continued slowly: "They just kicked us a bit and walked on by. Some of the fellows were wounded, but nobody was killed, though it was really a miracle. Had you been there, you and the students would have been in the next room over. That room was really blown up. The steel bunks were badly mangled from the explosions, and I doubt that you would have survived. No telling what they would have done, your being an American woman, either dead or alive . . . and the students——"

Again his voice trailed off into silence. He shifted his feet, then continued: "Oh, thank God you weren't there. Lady, you would have been killed." His voice dropped. He jingled the keys in his pocket a moment, searching for words that somehow didn't come out.

"Good-bye, Miss Bennett. I'll contact you later and see if we can reschedule this immunization program when things cool off a bit." With a nod of his head he jumped into his waiting jeep and drove away.

I watched the jeep lurch out the gate and onto the main street. Then I turned around and walked slowly back to the nursing school. God seemed extremely near as I pushed open the screen door to my office and sat down at my desk. The pile of work somehow seemed bearable.

The Tet Holiday

The Tet holiday was the biggest occasion of the year for the Vietnamese. One could compare it to our Christmas, New Year, Thanksgiving, and Easter all rolled into one. Businesses closed for three or four days, and the whole country celebrated. Prior to the holiday, people blocked off some of the downtown streets and transformed them into brilliant flower markets. Yellow and purple chrysanthemums, pink and red roses, and bundles of fresh multicolored pastel gladiolus all stood side by side, almost choking each other. For weeks the tailoring business flourished. Everyone donned new clothes during the festive season. Delicacies and other food filled the markets in preparation for the multitude of feasts.

The yearly vacation from school took place during Tet. Naturally, the students all wanted to go home. I was glad to see vacation come but sad to see the students all leave. Since some of them came from areas controlled by the VC, I never could be sure that all the girls would be able to return. Several did return to school late. One chubby student excitedly described her fright when caught in cross fire. Another girl reported how the VC had surrounded her village for several days, and she had been unable to escape until late one night when she discovered the guard asleep. Still another tearfully stated that for the second time in two years Communist rockets had destroyed her parents' home. The girls made such valiant efforts to return to school. Their eagerness to learn amazed me. I would gladly have used every available excuse to delay my return to Loma Linda during my school days; not so with them. Nothing short of their own death kept them at home following vacation—and none of them died.

In honor of Tet, colorful decorations of red, blue, green, yellow, and silver brightened the streets. The markets teemed with eager throngs buying gifts and general supplies. The students begged me to take them riding through the streets of Saigon in the mission truck so they could view the sights. We would pack as many as thirty-five girls into the back of the van or pickup, and off we'd charge after study hour at night.

It seemed as though all the millions in Saigon decided to sight-see the same nights that we chose. Needless to say, the normal Saigon congestion seemed like the wide-open spaces of Texas in comparison to Tet traffic. I'd inch our way along in the truck, being especially careful to watch out for the swarms of Hondas that jumped and sputtered around me. Sometimes five people jammed themselves on one small motorcycle. The two-mile ride to the center of the city took as long as an hour because of the crowds. But the girls didn't seem to mind, and they passed the time singing lustily. Finally, I'd park the truck in some alley and let the students roam the streets, marketplaces, and flower stalls. They were in ecstacy.

One morning during vacation, a student invited me to her home as a guest at her family's Tet feast. She even let me assist the women in preparing the food. I chopped up bits of onion, mushroom, cabbage, and numerous other ingredients, pressed the combination into little oblong shapes, and wrapped thin white sheets of rice paper around them. Then we fried the little log-shaped delicacies until crispy golden brown and served them with a sauce made of rotten fish called *nuc-mom*. Finally, after several hours of work, the feast lay completed. It was delicious—including the rotten fish sauce. (I'm a culinary adventuress, though ordinarily a vegetarian.)

The men sat at one long table while the women and children devoured their food in the kitchen. Since I was a guest, though, they sat me at the head of the table alongside the aged grandfather. Then, seated on the other side of me and across the table were two American men, both about fifteen years my senior. My student had thoughtfully decided I might be more comfortable if someone else who spoke my language was present at her Tet feast. Her older sister happened to be a room maid at the local hotel that housed American civilian construction workers. Evidently the nursing student prevailed upon her to invite some men home for dinner so her teacher would have someone with whom to talk.

Buddha's birthday was another school holiday, out of respect for the Buddhist students. One of them again invited me as her guest for the festive day. The two of us roared all over Saigon on her Suzuki, visiting several different Buddhist temples. She explained the various prayer procedures and other religious rituals to the best of her ability. Then we ate dinner with the Buddhist priests at her own temple. It was a fascinating experience. The priests and I could not communicate verbally, so we smiled at each other as we lifted our chopsticks to devour the delicious feast.

Another time a student begged me to join her at a certain hotel for a "special program." "I invite you my special guest, *Co* Bennett," she almost shouted in her excitement. Naively, I accepted, not asking any further questions about it. That particular evening I innocently found myself sitting on the front row, a guest of honor, at a strip show for the American servicemen hotel clients. She thought I would enjoy the performance immensely because the other Americans did, and I was an American. To her way of thinking, it was a special treat for me. It would have been terribly rude for me to walk out in disgust, so I sat quietly beside her, asking myself, "Help! What do I do now? How can I witness here? After all, I am a missionary!" Later that evening I explained as tactfully as I could that Christians ordinarily don't attend such "special programs."

I always enjoyed visiting my students' homes. One of them once asked me to join her family, saying, "My mother, she very good cooker. Please come eat my house." Gladly I accepted. After the scrumptious Vietnamese meal, the girl took me for a walk through the crowded alley she called home. Suddenly we found ourselves nearly crushed by scores of children—her neighbors. It must have been preplanned—I don't know for certain—but they all started jabbering at once. My hostess implored me to sing some Vietnamese songs for them. Well, singing is just not one of my special talents. But I couldn't be a polite guest and refuse an Oriental request. So I sang all the Vietnamese songs I knew. Fortunately for the audience, my repertoire was limited. Then the children besieged me with requests for "American songs." I complied. There in the gutter of that alley, completely surrounded by the crowd of little children, their older siblings, and parents, I attempted to sing "Old MacDonald Had a Farm" and "Way Down Upon the Swanee River." Finally I ended my concert with "Jesus Loves the Little Children" and "Jesus Loves Me." No professional musician could have been more enthusiastically applauded.

The Vietnamese like to sing. A musically gifted Vietnamese worker and Filipino missionary organized the nurses into a choir. The two talented people brought harmonious chords from the girls' untrained voices. The student choir performed at various church meetings and even took part in a city-wide music festival once. Sometimes the military chaplains at the bases surrounding Saigon invited the girls to sing for the GI Sunday services.

I'd pack them into the back of our red mission truck and

drive them to the bases. During one singing appointment, I noticed some GI's climbing on top of their barracks to watch our loaded truck come grinding up the hill in low gear. The fellows whistled and shouted a warm welcome. Another time the GI's of Long Binh Army Post donated $2,000 to our nursing school. Their gift made it possible to purchase much-needed anatomical models, charts, and textbooks which the school did not have. Those men will never know how much we appreciated it, though the concert didn't quite rate that high a fee. God certainly provided well for us.

"No, Co Bennett, Please Don't Go"

Life went on with its busy routine of teaching and supervision of students at the hospital. Seldom did I have an uninteresting moment. No one at the mission had much time to even consider pleasure. Sometimes I longed to escape the restrictions of the city and compound walls. The nursing students nurtured the same feelings. But we couldn't do much about the situation.

There wasn't even a place away from the city safe enough for us to have a simple outdoor picnic. To compensate for our confinement, we became excited over simple pleasures such as trips to the local Saigon zoo. But afterward I'd feel sad because the poor animals looked so thin and sickly. One particular bear seemed to become skinnier by the week, and his ribs stuck out so that it was quite obvious there couldn't be anything underneath that dilapidated furry coat except an empty chasm. His brown eyes pierced one with a dull, dejected glare, and occasionally he uttered a mournful cry that chilled one's spine. At times I actually wanted to cry with him in sympathy. One day I didn't see the bear anymore, and somehow I was relieved, yet sorrowful. Even at the zoo, constant reminders of the presence of war loomed around us. Large rolls of barbed wire surrounded the entire area, spilling out into the nearby streets. Beside the barbed-wire barricades stood large white signs in three languages that almost screamed out at the passersby: Danger! Mines Implanted Here! Yet some people sauntered by nonchalantly. Little Vietnamese children scampered in and around the area, and American servicemen paused briefly to adjust the focus on their cameras for that perfect shot.

While the zoo was not the world's most pleasant place, it did have some beauty spots. A picturesque lily pond lay right in the center of the park. It was complete with bright red bridge and Oriental teahouse and banked by thick green grass—so much fun to lie on and dream about home. Then directly across the cement sidewalk stood an archaic, pagodalike museum that possessed ancient Vietnamese art treasures and pieces of historical interest. It was fascinating to wander through the high-ceilinged room and try to imagine what Vietnam had once been like. And, of course, the brown Saigon River—bordered by rows of stately green palm trees—lazily glided by. So the students and I tried to content ourselves with small, safe pleasures such as our zoo trips.

Finally there dawned a glorious day when we found out it would be safe to take a jaunt to Vung Tau, the beach town that lay on the coast of the South China Sea about sixty miles away. Until now, the VC had spasmodically controlled the road to Vung Tau. They frequently blew up United States military convoys and shot down helicopters flying over the area. So naturally, civilians involving Americans stayed out of that traffic, and this included even beach-loving me. Excitement soared when we discovered that the road was secure once again.

Eagerly the students and I made beach plans for the next Sunday. Saturday night they thronged to my apartment for a "going-to-the-beach-tomorrow" party. But we retired early to be fresh for the big day ahead. Sunday morning, incessant banging at my front door woke me up well ahead of schedule. I grabbed my blue robe, threw it around me, and ran to the door.

There stood a group of my students gazing sadly into my now-startled face. Instead of happy smiles, their faces carried traces of dried-up tears. Nervously they fingered the buttons on their white blouses. Then they all started talking loudly.

"*Co* Bennett. Oh! *Co* Bennett!" Dead silence followed. Words seemed to stick in their throats. Ushering them into my apartment, I joined them on the floor—we always communicated best when sitting there. Finally a tall girl with big brown eyes began to speak. The words came faster and faster, so rapidly I could hardly understand her. "*Co* Bennett, you must not go to Vung Tau today. You must not go today. Please, please don't go today."

"But, why don't you want me to go?" A giant question mark covered my whole face. The students noticed it, but again their words just wouldn't come. "You were so excited about going just last night. Whatever has happened to change your mind?"

She gazed at me disconsolately and slowly, almost painfully, voiced her answer. "Last night I dreamed that if you went to Vung Tau today, the VC would capture you and kill you. Please don't go. We don't want anything to happen to you." Suddenly her eyes flooded with tears, and the sobs of the other students echoed in the room.

Their concern for my welfare touched me but somewhat irritated me at the same time. It had been a year since I had been close to a beach. Why should some dream keep me from a long-awaited jaunt? It had been weeks since I had even had a day off, much less had a chance for escape from the crushing captivity of crowded, war-torn Saigon. Disappointment crept over me. Trying to retain a semblance of composure, I replied, "Now, students, many times we have bad dreams, but that doesn't mean they come true. Remember, the army officers told us that it would be safe to travel. Are you sure you don't want me to go?"

The students' tears came faster now. The answer

reverberated through my apartment. "No. You must not go. No. You must not go, *Co* Bennett. We do not want to go either. We will not go."

"OK! OK! Students, we won't go if you really don't want to." With that they picked themselves up off the floor and shuffled down the dark hall, then down the stairs, and outside to their dormitory. Sunday turned out to be just another day of work, with buzzing helicopters overhead and colossal traffic jams outside the gate.

But Monday did not turn out to be a usual day. Early in the morning I turned on the radio and listened to the reports of battles from the previous day—helicopters shot down, convoys blown up throughout Vietnam, and soldiers killed. The voice of the announcer droned on. Suddenly the words *Vung Tau* came over the air. I listened closely. "Early Sunday morning the road to Vung Tau was recaptured by the Communist forces following several battles in the area. Five convoys were blown up from implanted road mines. Roadblocks were set up all along the highway by the VC, and all civilian vehicles were stopped. The occupants of the vehicles were taken out and shot beside the road. It has also been reported that many Vietnamese civilians were killed or wounded due to the hostile activity on the Vung Tau highway, . . . yesterday . . ."

The announcer continued with the rest of the news, but I didn't hear any more. By now my knees shook and I fell limply beside my bed. This time *my* eyes shed tears, and all my sobbing voice could whisper was simply, "Thank You, God, for protecting me once again."

The Men in a Missionary's Life

Ordinarily one doesn't think of missionary nurses having men in their lives. I know some people feel that they are something the single missionary woman arbitrarily relinquishes the minute she accepts the position. But let me tell you a secret—we single missionaries happen to be human too. However, I must admit that I had some of those thoughts whirling in the back of my mind. When I made my decision between Saigon and Mark, I never considered the possibility that other men might enter my life during my mission term. I didn't give a great deal of thought to the presence of the 550,000 American men in Vietnam at that time or to what my relationship to some of them would be. I was a missionary. Missionaries don't have social life, and that was that!

Every Sabbath as the GI's poured into the compound, clad in their green suits and black jungle boots, I at first tried to stay my distance from them. No one was ever going to accuse me of coming to Vietnam to socialize. I had come to work!

In fact, I guess I must have been so cool toward them that the other missionaries encouraged me to befriend the lonely men—so I did. Some needed mothers, it seemed. Others wanted a sister-type friendship. Still others, I discovered, hoped for a more-involved relationship than I could honestly give. I learned that one could not be all things to all people.

In the meantime, Mark and I communicated regularly for several months. But gradually we started growing apart. Though he may not have intended it that way, I interpreted ultimatums in between the lines of his letters. I understood his dilemma—he was graduating soon and wanted his life settled.

But my conscience refused to allow me to leave the infant nursing school at a crucial time in its development when I didn't feel I knew Mark well enough to commit my life to him forever. We wrote volumes and sent yards of tapes across the ten thousand miles separating us. Mixed feelings battled within me. I pleaded with God for guidance. He answered. Finally, with sadness, I released Mark from the unspoken obligation to concentrate his emotional energy in my direction.

One day, months later, I received a letter from him telling me that he would be getting married soon. Again I swirled within. Feeling almost crushed in spite of my decision, I cried. Yet gradually I felt a quiet stability rising within. I was happy for him. He wanted companionship, and now he would have it. Through the past months I had learned to respect him deeply. Our friendship had been beneficial, and I honestly cared enough about him to want the best for him. Recognizing that our life-styles were not identical, I realized that someone else could perhaps bring him greater happiness. For months we had both prayed about the relationship. Quite obviously God had someone else in mind for Mark. I must wait to see where He would lead me. Intellectually, I knew it was God's will.

Still, for many days I allowed sadness to drench my spirit. Sometimes my soul cried out, almost bitterly, "God, if I'm an old maid because of Your bringing me here to Vietnam . . . I'll . . . I'll be so mad." Back in a secluded corner of my mind I kept halfway expecting God miraculously to give marriage to me as a present—my reward for Vietnam. It was somewhat like my saying, "OK, God, I'm being a good girl. I came here to the mission field and left all those chances back home. Now when are You going to give me my lollipop?"

In time, my dread of singleness vanished. I learned to cope with life myself. And when God finally leads me to a companion, fear of loneliness, desperation, or social pressure will not taint my love for him. Though it would not be my first choice, if God sees in His great wisdom that it is best for me not to have a husband, that I can serve Him through a career, then that too is all right.

But many tearful moments occurred back in Vietnam when I received wedding invitations and baby announcements from my nursing classmates and other close friends. Yet at the same time God came especially close. His peace filled me. I had tried to be willing to let Him lead my life completely. Right now He needed me in Vietnam.

Every Sabbath we missionaries fixed a huge dinner for all the soldiers who came in from the outlying bases. Sometimes we had seventy servicemen, and then some Sabbaths only seven. We never knew how many would come, as attendance at church depended on the war. Sabbath mornings the GI's would come rolling in through the compound gates in jeeps, borrowed officers' sedans, pickups, trucks, and army ambulances—the only vehicle the medics could secure—or on motorcycles. Others took buses, hitchhiked, or flew into Ton Son Nhut via helicopter.

My job Sabbath morning involved fixing breakfast for the early-bird soldiers who happened to arrive well before church. It was fun. Since I never knew if four or forty-four would show up, it was a challenge. The fellows always helped me, though. We'd make piles of pancakes or fry or scramble dozens of eggs while they drank gallons of Tang or reconstituted powdered milk enriched with canned milk. Fortunately we missionaries had commissary privileges at the American military food store, where we procured American foods at discount prices. Food in the local native markets was exorbitantly priced. Every day, but especially on Fridays when we shopped for the weekend, I thanked God for our commissary privileges.

Sabbath afternoons most of the fellows had to head back to their bases. But if some had permission from their officers to stay longer, the GI's piled into my apartment for "rap sessions." They'd talk for hours about home, their girl friends, wives, problems in their barracks, their officers, and life in general. Then we missionaries invited them to our homes for little parties after sundown. We'd fix big bowls of popcorn and play table games.

My work schedule didn't allow for much social life, although plenty was available if I'd had more hours in the day to enjoy it. However, I do have happy memories of dinners at some lovely restaurants. One time an army doctor stationed at the Third Field Army Hospital just up the street from the mission asked my medical director if he could take me out for dinner. Fortunately my superior agreed quite heartily. It turned out to be quite an occasion, because four doctors escorted me to the officers' dining room that evening rather than just one. I hardly knew how to act, since I had never been to dinner with four men before. They picked me up in their open jeep. Each man carried a rifle, and onlookers from peaceful countries would have thought I was an escaped convict under armed escort.

Looking back over my Vietnam experiences, I realize how wonderful the GI's were to me. They often purchased little gifts for me—especially on their R and R's. My belongings still include a piece of silk from Bangkok, souvenirs from Hong Kong, Singapore, and Hawaii, as well as from Sydney a dear toy koala bear wearing a pink ribbon. Sometimes the pockets of their green fatigues bulged with little things to cheer me.

Vietnam was definitely a man's world, and I became tired of the continual masculine environment. If I merely set my foot outside the compound gate, various versions of wolf whistles, shouts, stares, and comments from the passing American military traffic greeted me. At first the attention was fun, I must admit; but as time passed, I grew weary of it. My GI friends seemed to understand and tried to protect me from such "harassment" when they were with me. They also realized how much I missed talking with girls my own age and being exposed to feminine frolic. They tried to make up for the lack by purchasing women's magazines from the military PX and then gallantly paging through them with me, patiently discussing my views or comments on dresses or dishes. Though a touch of tomboy definitely lurks in me, I have my lace-perfume-ruffles-china-crystal facets too. The men understood, and they allowed and encouraged me to express that side of my personality as well. To all you Vietnam veterans: a great big Thank you for showering me with so much kindness. I'll always remember you.

One of the Adventist GI's I came to know especially well. He helped me fix those early morning Sabbath breakfasts, and I didn't have one nonfunctioning item in my apartment, thanks to his mechanical talents. We enjoyed a warm friendship during the eight remaining months he had in Vietnam. When on Friday evenings he came into Saigon from his outlying base and I had a spare moment, we discussed a wide gamut of subjects that enlarged my perspective on life. He gave me continued encouragement, mingled with a certain bit of admiration, that steadied and "re-self-confidenced" my sometimes faltering ego. He and I laughed a lot together. As we shared dozens of cyclo and motorcycle rides through Saigon's mad traffic, he'd lean over and shout above the vehicle din surrounding us, "You've got to be the neatest person in the world—you're never afraid."

Our adventure-loving natures sometimes overworked our guardian angels, no doubt. But we didn't purposely flirt with danger. We simply became so totally absorbed in our zest for the unearthing of new places and people that we forgot the possible presence of an enemy.

One Saturday night we set out to discover something new. Up to now our downtown jaunts had consisted mainly of finding new restaurants or wandering around the streets people-watching, since the multitude of bars and discotheques didn't appeal to us. That particular evening we sauntered along the Saigon docks, observing the night life of the river people. Up until then our sampan rides had always been in daylight, since the boatmen didn't venture out with them after dark. But suddenly we noticed a larger sampan filling with people.

"Look, the people are paying," I said. "It must be a ferry. Let's get on and see where it goes. How come we never noticed it before when we've been down here?" The full tropical moon shimmered down on the Saigon River, splashing the tiny ripples with silver hues and bathing the whole atmosphere in a sparkling radiance.

"It's a perfect night for a boat ride," my escort replied. "Let's hop on." He grasped my hand firmly, and together we ran down to the landing, dodging children and jumping over baskets of fish in our haste. Gingerly we stepped into the boat and sat down, crushed in by our Vietnamese fellow passengers and their baskets of long French bread and stinking fish. Our debut seemed to cause quite a stir as all eyes turned on us. The chattering suddenly increased two hundredfold. The ride was delightful. The wooden barge churned into the gentle waves and quickly crossed the river. On our arrival, my escort paid our fare and we disembarked.

Then we set out to explore. It was a typical Vietnamese village complete with little shops, a marketplace, and multitudes of people milling around. We strolled by little tumbledown shacks made of empty, flattened-out beer cans. The shacks stood "sardined" together in uneven rows, lining the chuckhole-filled dirt road. The doors all stood open, and on

the floors families sat eating their evening meals. As we
passed, the children and adults rushed to the doors and
windows to peer out. Quite obviously, Caucasians infrequently
visited the village. Yet everyone smiled warmly, and the
children nearly smothered us with their affection. Stopping on a
wooden bridge, we looked out across the darkness to the
flickering lights of Saigon framed by occasional bursts of
gigantic orange-and-red clouds, flashing brilliantly in the night
sky—the aftermath of explosions from some distant fire fight.
We stood enraptured with the beauty of the scene.

Suddenly a well-dressed Vietnamese stepped up directly
behind us and politely tapped my escort on the arm. Quickly he
started speaking fast, immaculate French. Understanding part
of what he said, I thanked him and blurted out to my friend,
"We've got to get out of here immediately. This place is
infested with VC. The man warned that it's extremely
dangerous for us to be here."

"OK, Babe, let's beat it." With that, we dashed back to the
dock, hand in hand. Since neither of us spoke Vietnamese with
any degree of fluency, we had not asked how often the boats
crossed over to the city or even if another boat went back that
night.

Occasionally our adventurous spirits needed subduing with
plain good judgment. But Someone much wiser than we had
provided for our safety. The last ferry of the night, so we
discovered, sat warming its motor for the return trip. We had
barely made it.

Then there was the evening we ate at a floating restaurant.
Right after we left, someone discovered a hidden time bomb
ready to explode in a sampan underneath it. Again God
protected.

Life never knew one boring minute when my friend was
around. He brought me great happiness. I must have had a
similar effect on him, for he always managed to find a way to

Saigon for a few minutes now and then, even if he wasn't supposed to be off base. On one occasion during an alert, he came to Saigon without permission, so his officers demoted him to the lowest rank. Feeling really bad about it, I begged him to stay on base until the restriction ended. In time he regained his rank, and we celebrated the occasion. A few times I journeyed out to visit him on his army post. My only method of transportation was by *lambretta,* a kiddie-car-like vehicle that seated six adults comfortably but usually carried fifteen passengers, together with chickens and children, well packed into the closed space. But I enjoyed the rides as long as I could wrangle an outside seat. Once when he was confined to the base on Sabbath, my fellow missionaries drove me out to his base, and we all spent Sabbath together in the army chapel and picnicked in the chaplain's office. (Military bases in war zones have no picnic facilities, in case you were wondering.)

When his Vietnam military tour ended, he invited me to accompany him in his processing-out procedures. Perhaps I'm the only American woman who assisted a GI with departure proceedings from Vietnam. Anyway, I received a lot of stares. When we finally said good-bye, I sobbed and sobbed. We both prayed about the future of our relationship.

Again our voluminous correspondence kept the mail service busy. Once again I had to grapple with the question of marriage. But simultaneously my mind fought another battle—a reassessment of values. The mission problems, coupled with the exposure to the gross inconsistencies of the war, completely uprooted my youthful idealism. My deep respect for political and church leadership wavered, a respect that had been ingrained within me since childhood. A silent cynicism mingled with bitterness threatened to engulf my spirit.

What did I want from life? I didn't know. My friend's highest goal was to spend his life as a missionary, and that had always been mine—till now. At the moment I was not even sure if I wanted to be a Seventh-day Adventist the rest of my life, much less a missionary. I felt the church had nothing to offer except continual confusion and conflict—something I wanted no part of. Somehow the thought chilled me when I considered spending the rest of my life cooped up inside compound walls that harbored strife and hostility. I couldn't lift my eyes above my particular situation to view the total world mission program and to see the joy that overseas service brings most missionaries.

My inner reluctance to deal with the administrative responsibilities in the nursing school intensified my unhappiness. At times I actually hated the leadership role I found myself in. I felt the church had completely taken advantage of me. Inwardly I rebelled. Using romance as an excuse to escape my own frustration over my position of responsibility and the problems of the compound, the temptation to leave almost overpowered me. Right then I longed for someone strong to turn to, someone to make my decisions for me. But I had to live with myself. No matter how I felt, no matter what happened, I would finish my term. There was no replacement for me anyway, and very deep inside I cared what happened to the nursing school and those students I loved. Choosing to face my turmoil, I would not run away from it.

I never shared my negative feelings toward the church and missions with anyone, so no one knew my psychological strife. The compound situation made it difficult for the missionaries to be close to each other. They don't have time to listen, and besides, they wouldn't understand, I told myself, and it would just aggravate the existing problems were I to unload my true feelings on my overworked co-workers.

As my thoughts raged within me, I knew that Vietnam was not the place in my life to consider the lifelong decision of marriage. Although I was quite fond of this man and missed him greatly, I could not honestly sort out my true feelings for him amid the other questions surging within. The tearful battle struggled within me for weeks. Finally I realized the only honest alternative was to end the relationship so that he could find someone more in tune with his aspirations. I could not ask him to change his life goal, and my feelings toward missions made it impossible for me to consider a lasting commitment to them.

Inwardly I struggled for quite a while. Why had God allowed my lifelong desire for overseas church service to shatter because of my exposure to mission life in war-torn Saigon with its pressures? Why couldn't the church and God have given me an easy, pleasant assignment in some peaceful place so that I wouldn't have to suffer the pangs of disillusionment alone? Just a year before, the relationship with Mark had ended because I believed Vietnam was where God wanted me. Now I grappled with the problem from the opposite viewpoint. But God had valuable lessons to teach me through the experience. As I searched for His peace, I found it; and He gave me a renewed stability. In time I accepted the challenge of missions positively once again, but that miracle didn't happen till after I left Vietnam.

Gradually I realized more than ever that marriage must involve the right time, the right person, and the right place—factors that Vietnam did not give me then. I still believed God was present in my life, and I sought His guidance and comfort. He pulled me through the crisis. Then I relaxed once again, realizing He would continue to lead. I knew He hadn't completely forgotten my desires—other opportunities for warm relationships would arise later. And I didn't need to feel pressured into making any immediate decisions about my future.

However, the GI and I are both thankful for our friendship. We gave each other happiness and stability during one of the most difficult periods of our lives—Vietnam. And I was genuinely happy for him when I received his wedding announcement two years later. Today we still remain good friends.

Life goes on in spite of heartaches, weariness, and frustration. My life in Vietnam offered occasional amusing and interesting events. Once I received a ride home to the mission in a twenty-ton army semitrailer. As the enormous vehicle chugged up to the gate, I discovered from my lofty perch high in the cab's front seat that the gatekeeper had gone. So I gingerly maneuvered myself down from the cab to open the gate for the truck, which took several munutes. In the meantime, the driver had to manipulate the vehicle at such a sharp angle to enter the mission compound that the truck and trailer completely blocked the whole street. Traffic piled up for a couple of blocks. Horns blared and engines raced impatiently. My first reaction to the congestion I was causing was that of embarrassment. Then I suddenly broke into laughter. Silently I apologized for the traffic jam while the giant truck rolled through the gate into the compound so it could turn around. My escort, the driver, laughed too.

At another time a GI friend and I had to hitchhike home to Saigon from the beach via an ammunition convoy when we missed the last chopper for the day. I would gladly have taken the Vietnamese bus home, but it was against military orders for American soldiers to ride civilian buses. Even now I still chuckle as I recall how he persuaded me to stand out on the road with my thumb protruding upward. He stood behind me, saying, "They'll stop for you long before they will for me. I've got to get back to the base before my pass expires. You've got to save my skin, Marilyn."

One day I happened to become acquainted with four-star General Abrams' private pilot, who gave me occasional rides in the general's plane when the chief was elsewhere. I also went on tours through the Ton Son Nhut radar center. Sometimes the men there let me direct the planes. The lingo didn't make much sense to my aviation-ignorant brain—"4732 over to 7635," but the specks on the scope changed position in answer to my command. The pilots answered in surprised tones as they recognized a woman's voice. Once I listened to the conversations between the control center and the crew of a B-52 bombing mission en route from Guam to the Cambodian battlefront. They even let me hear the countdown as the bombers reached their target—some North Vietnamese headquarters deep in a Cambodian jungle. A radarscope showed the bombs dropping, and I watched with interest. But bombing raids made me sad.

Other unusual activities included finding myself the only soprano for the *Messiah* presentation in a sea of basses, tenors, and a few alto army nurses. The pathetic thing is that I don't claim to be a singer in the first place. I merely answered the pleas of an army radio announcer for sopranos. Finally, to my great comfort, two other sopranos showed up for the grand finale.

Then one time I flew up to a large army base at Qui Nhon in the central part of Vietnam, escorting a nine-year-old deaf Vietnamese boy who was to have audiological testing. It turned out to be an interesting experience for both of us. We did not communicate verbally at all, but the child was extremely obedient. Missionaries in Vietnam had military-transport privileges, and whenever a woman flew on one of the troop planes, she always received an invitation to sit with the pilots and navigators in the cockpit. Thuan, the nine-year-old, accompanied me to the cockpit and especially enjoyed watching the pilots firsthand.

Part of one flight took place at night, and the explosions underneath us were quite visible. From the air the battles were actually rather beautiful and resembled fireworks on the Fourth of July. We saw the tracer bullets flying through the air hundreds of feet below. Over a set of earphones I listened to the conversations between the control towers and pilots. I particularly paid attention as they guided our flights away from dangerous areas. Then the plane set down at one military camp to let off some troops who had just arrived in the country. Clad in their fresh green fatigues and shiny black jungle boots, the men disembarked as I watched from the cockpit, and I wondered how they felt about their new assignment. The earphones still rested on my head, and I casually listened to the remarks the control tower personnel made. Suddenly the voice from the tower deepened its pitch and sternly advised the aircraft commander to leave the airfield immediately: "There is a possibility the base may be attacked in the next few minutes. We urge you to become airborne immediately."

The plane instantly lunged forward. Never had I ridden on a plane which took off so abruptly. Despite the fact that our seat belts were fastened, I had to grasp the edge of the seat with one hand and grab Thuan with the other to keep from hurtling forward. I observed the look of relief on the faces of the crew when we attained cruising altitude. Strangely enough I wasn't the least bit frightened. No doubt existed in my mind but that the angels would protect that plane. And they did.

The only Seventh-day Adventist army nurse in Vietnam at that time, Claudia Caflin, was stationed at Qui Nhon. She and I had a wonderful time together that weekend.

I learned that I was the first American civilian woman other than entertainers to visit the 45,000-man base. Consequently I received a "general's welcome." One of the most interesting aspects of my visit involved a tour to the VC ward of the 85th Evacuation Hospital. The men there had never seen an American civilian woman, and their response was so warm I nearly suffocated. I can still hear those prisoners shouting, "Number One, Number One" as I walked by. ("Number One" was a high compliment in the vernacular of the Vietnamese who had been around the GI's.) It was hard to believe the friendly men were my supposed "enemy."

On Sabbath Claudia and I had a simple church service with the Adventist GI's stationed in the area, then we fixed them a vegetarian meal and invited some of the officers to join us. All the men warmly appreciated our culinary attempts.

Claudia worked in the emergency room. I accompanied her to it one morning. And while there, the ambulance brought in an eighteen-year-old GI whose eyes had just been partially blown out by a grenade explosion. He was fully alert. As he heard the voices of us assisting the doctors, his face brightened in spite of his pain. I still hear his plaintive cry, "Oh! Oh! It's been *so* long since I've heard American women's voices. You sound beautiful. Please come talk to me. Could you just . . . just touch my hand . . . just for a minute?"

Since I was merely observing and not really involved with emergency-room routine that morning, I went over and stood beside him. Then I placed my hand in his. It was ice cold even though the atmosphere was warm. I could tell he was frightened. His facial muscles twitched with pain, but he was trying hard to be brave. I talked to him until they wheeled him away to surgery. Why did war have to exist? Why did people have to deliberately slaughter each other? Such questions often churned around and around within me.

Another excursion that particular weekend consisted of a sampan ride to a small rocky island in the South China Sea. A small group of officers accompanied Claudia and me on the swimming and skin-diving spree. The tropical underwater vegetation was intricate in its perfection. I was really happy to have the opportunity to see the lush underworld firsthand. After Sunday on the island, a captain invited us to his ship for dinner. Navy patrol boats took us out to its anchorage in the Qui Nhon Harbor. The evening was delightful. Claudia and I had many interesting opportunities to talk about our church and its world mission as the officers asked us countless questions. We did our best to witness effectively.

Every once in a while a woman has a special experience that leaves her with such happy feelings about her femininity that it steadies her over the rougher times. One Friday my superiors decided I should fly to Danang for Sabbath to meet with the church members there. Since we missionaries had military transportation privileges, I decided to save money and use an air-force plane rather than fly Air Vietnam, the civilian transport. Always ready for travel, I was excited as I walked into the military waiting area on Ton Son Nhut Air Base that Friday morning.

Quickly I glanced around to observe my fellow travelers. GI's fairly well filled the room, but I noticed one other American woman seated in the center. She had a couple guitar cases beside her, and from her appearance I decided she must be an entertainer for the troops. Her long bleached platinum hair, heavily teased, stood high above her flawless face that seemed packed with thick makeup. Wearing a low-cut micromini dress and high boots, she sat smoking, with her legs crossed at the knees.

Many times GI's surrounded us American women in Vietnam whenever we went out in public. It was rather like being celebrities, and we came to expect some attention wherever we went. But that morning I quickly concluded that the men weren't likely to want to talk to a missionary when they had an opportunity to fraternize with a night-club singer. I was too shy to go sit near her or speak to her, though I thought it would be interesting. So I quietly walked to the rear of the room, sat down as inconspicuously as possible, and immediately pulled out from the tote bag a stack of papers to grade.

After a few minutes, I looked up and noticed a group of men sitting around me. Before long we were chatting freely. They wanted to know what I was doing in Vietnam. I told them, and soon they asked questions about Seventh-day Adventist missions. I glanced over at my fellow female traveler to see what crowd she had attracted. Expecting the whole room to have flocked around her, I nearly collapsed when I saw the empty seats beside her. Suddenly our eyes met. I felt her gaze on me—cold, glaring, envious, yet it looked lonely, and I wished I'd gone to sit beside her. The men interpreted our nonverbal communication instantly and chuckled.

Right then the plane came, ending our conversation abruptly. A Phantom-jet-fighter pilot picked up my tote bag, and we walked together toward the plane. Just as we reached the stair ramp, he turned to me and said, "You know, we men don't get to talk to American women very often. About the only ones we see are the entertainers. Having the opportunity to talk to someone like you is a real treat—you're a special kind of person." My spirits really soared as the plane climbed into the sky.

One rewarding friendship in Vietnam involved an air-force sergeant whom I shall call Allen. When we first became acquainted, he vowed that his philosophical beliefs embraced agnosticism. I must admit that I considered him a challenge, since my sheltered upbringing precluded contacts with people whose religious beliefs conflicted with mine. He came to the mission frequently, and we spent much time discussing our positions on God. As time went on, I noticed him soften. We became close friends, and he helped in numerous activities on the mission, even occasionally teaching a children's Sabbath School class. Also we played clarinet duets for church, and he faithfully taught an English class to the nursing students. At his request, we started having worships and praying together. During my limited free time, we read the Bible and discussed the Sabbath. Though our friendship was never serious, one day he made the statement that he intended to marry an

Adventist girl someday. And when he returned to the States, he did just that. Later he wrote me about his baptism. I was really excited. Then when I returned home, I saw him with his wife at a friend's wedding. We chatted for quite a while afterward, reviewing Vietnam. As I turned to leave, Allen touched my arm gently and said, "Marilyn, thank you for showing me the right way. . . . Thank you for everything you did for me in Vietnam."

At that instant his wife embraced me and softly whispered, "I also want to thank you for what you did. Allen has made me a better Adventist." I felt a lump in my throat. Perhaps men did have a purpose in missionaries' lives after all.

Ruthita

"Oh, Marilyn! I've got exciting news for you," the missionary's wife bubbled. "A student missionary from Union College is coming to help out with the hospital immunization program. It's a 'she' this time. [Up to then most of the student missionaries to the Far East had been men.] Isn't that wonderful! Here this whole year you've been by yourself—now you'll have companionship. Union calls her their 'Blonde Bomb for Vietnam.' At least we know she is blonde. We've also received word that she's very talented and vivacious."

Genuine eagerness sparkled from the blue eyes of the little woman facing me. The midafternoon sun beamed down on her short hair, radiating a halo of brilliance above her. To me she was an angel in flesh. The tenderness of her personality engulfed me. Her daintiness, mingled with a certain dynamic effervescence, reminded me of my own mother. She understood what the pressure of responsibility, mingled with the continual conflict on the mission compound, had done to my carefree spirit—not that we'd talked that much. Little time existed in either of our schedules for such luxuries. But she grasped my feelings and cared. Once when discouragement mirrored itself on my face, she sent her servant over to my apartment with one of her favorite tropical plants and a cheery note. I loved her.

Looking into her smile, I replied, "Oh, I am excited! Isn't that great! It'll be so good to have someone closer to my age here. I can hardly wait. When is she coming?"

"I don't know exactly, but it should be soon, so my husband says." She patted my arm affectionately, then walked on.

A few weeks later, Ruthita, the student missionary, arrived. Her blonde curly hair in contrast to my straight, short brown tresses made me a bit envious. The vibrance of her effervescent personality overshadowed my quietness. In many respects we were almost opposites. She stood tall. I was short. Her self-confident aggressiveness in tackling her waiting tasks was quite unlike the shrinking manner in which I had limped through my first days. For example, she valiantly drove the mission truck out into Saigon's terrible traffic her second day in Vietnam. It took me four months to muster up courage to nose the truck gingerly out the gate. (But then I never have enjoyed driving and am always willing to forgo the "pleasure.")

Her buoyant cheerfulness brought the compound fresh joy. Though younger than I, she taught me many valuable lessons of life—such as self-confidence, optimism, and assurance. In the ten months we shared the same narrow bedroom, only once can I recall our personality differences causing contention—and that one time was my fault. I apologized, and she forgave. We became quite close, and to this day we remain good friends.

Ruthita's official title read: Director, Immunization Program, Saigon Adventist Hospital. But let me back up a minute. Orphanages, schools, and refugee camps begged our hospital to immunize their children against DPT (diphtheria, pertussis, commonly called whooping cough, and tetanus), typhoid, cholera, plague, and polio. The hospital made strenuous efforts to treat as many as possible. Two or three of us would immunize several hundred children in an afternoon as well as try to keep up with the rest of the work load. But soon the requests mushroomed to the extent that it was impossible for our limited staff to handle the load. Our hospital was one of the few organizations in the Saigon area giving immunizations. So the administration asked the General Conference for a student missionary to take over the operation. Ruthita came in response to the request.

She dauntlessly jaunted all over Saigon and into the outlying villages in a little white Datsun station wagon furnished by the hospital, immunizing thousands of children. Much of the time she used a black injector gun operated by electricity. It was supposedly faster, safer, and more efficient than giving shots by needle. But many of the places where she held clinics were primitive, and no source of power for the gun existed, so she became an expert with the hypo as well.

She returned home in the afternoons filled with exciting tales of her adventures in "shooting children." Sometimes the military accompanied her to refugee camps where they injected as many as two thousand people in one day.

One time an American civilian doctor associated with a children's foundation asked her to accompany him by army helicopter to some far-flung area to inoculate several hundred refugee children. It turned out to be a rather hazardous venture because fighting disrupted their plans. On the return flight to Saigon, one of the chopper crew members turned to her, and pointing out the open side, matter-of-factly stated, "See those bodies lying on the ground below?—they're VC. We shot them on the way down." My roommate seemed especially grateful to be home again that afternoon.

For over a year I had enjoyed being the only single American girl at the mission, and now Ruthita suddenly overshadowed me. At times, I must admit, I became jealous of my unusually talented roommate. I envied the magnetic charm of her personality, her striking looks, the attention she attracted, the wide range of publicity given her—such as a ten-minute TV coverage of her immunization program on the CBS national network. I felt myself fading away into the background because of her effervescence.

Again the Lord had a lesson for me. Jealousy was one of the hardest things I'd ever dealt with—it was a situation that I had to struggle over on my knees. It involved a type of psychological pain that one cannot really explain, except that I know from personal experience the toll that the twins of jealousy and self-pity take on personal happiness. But with God's help, a grateful contentedness with life filled me. My silent transformation didn't happen overnight though—it took months of diligent effort. Actually, it wasn't until after I'd left Vietnam that the triumph finally became a reality. The jealousy left. Ordinarily God doesn't give us all striking personalities or beauty, but as a result of my Vietnam experiences I now stand much more confident in my inner strength, willing to face life squarely with no apologies, because God is my partner and He continues to sustain me. Some people learn such lessons in childhood. Others, like myself, mature a bit later.

A couple of years afterward, I drove nearly two thousand miles to Ruthita's wedding. The night before the ceremony we stayed up till three o'clock reminiscing about Vietnam—an odd subject for a bride-to-be to discuss on her wedding eve. She was a radiant bride, beautiful and charming as ever. I'm sure I was almost as proud of her as her mother and father were. Furthermore, there wasn't an atom of envy or jealousy within me. I felt myself overflowing with happiness for her.

Back in Vietnam, Ruthita and I had wonderful times. We stayed up till the wee hours of the morning discussing the multitude of men around us, the men back home, the mission, what we wanted from life, philosophy, religion, music, literature, and clothes. Together we discovered cozy Vietnamese, Chinese, and French restaurants all over the city. And the two of us rode helicopters, jeeps, and even Sherman tanks.

Leisurely we strolled the crowded markets looking for souvenirs. Sometimes flocks of children followed us, along with four or five GI's. Once during a monsoon downpour a small flash flood hit the market. We waded through muddy water up to our knees, having a delightful time, till a family of huge rats swam our way. Terrified, we shrieked and splashed everyone in sight in our haste to escape from the creatures. I'll never forget the looks and laughter coming from the *mamasans* surrounding us as we fled the market.

Then I remember the rides in the wooden sampans down the Saigon River. It was perhaps one of our favorite activities. The little boats chugged in and around the harbor through the maze of oceangoing vessels that constantly brought in fresh supplies of war materials. New jeeps or tanks would line their decks. We'd watch the huge cranes unload the ships. The Saigon River wound lazily around in huge curves which the little boats followed. On past the harbor area stood clusters of tiny tumbledown shacks hugging the riverbank. As we rode by, we could clearly see the pigs wallowing in the mud around them. The pigs would enter the houses and plop in the middle of the floor, nearly covering it, and the children and adults stepped around them. Viewing life from the river, one noticed things not visible by land.

Sometimes U.S. Navy patrol boats stopped our sampans, and the GI's pulled Ruthita and me into their "steel skimmers" with words of caution: "We don't want anything to happen to you dames out there—you'd better come ride with us!" Traveling the river Vietnamese style or via military made no difference to us—each method had its advantages or disadvantages.

Ruthita never had an unoccupied moment either. She taught English at such diverse places as a Catholic convent, a Buddhist orphanage, and our own Adventist nursing school. In addition she gave Bible studies to both Catholic and Buddhist priests and nuns. Her charm captured everyone. The GI's especially loved to talk to her.

My servant, Chi Hai, was just like a grandmother to us. Her wrinkled smile illuminated our busy days. She fixed the most delicious Oriental soups and dishes imaginable. And she even carefully sewed us several sets of matching dresses. We both loved her. The dear old woman must have hated cats, yet she nurtured our retine of felines with a toleration bordering heroism. I had three cats, a gift from a student. Then Ruthita discovered a litter of four kittens in a garbage heap. Tenderly she brought them home, which made a total of seven animals occupying our apartment. Ruthita woke herself up all during the night at three-hour intervals to feed the tiny scrawny creatures with a dropper. But soon they died, leaving us with our original cat family of Ruth, Naomi, and Boaz.

We girls took our share of the compound entertaining as long as Chi Hai managed the cuisine. Scores of GI's and passing missionaries, tourists, and union and division officers from Singapore graced our table. On one occasion a host of guests filled the living room, waiting for Chi Hai to fry the last rice and tofu patty. Suddenly my cat Boaz lunged into the center of the room carrying a large mouse. Not expecting to find so many visitors, he dropped his prey momentarily. My surprised guests—ministers from Singapore attending mission committee meetings—politely lifted their feet to let the cat and mouse pass unobstructed. Ruthita and I scrambled up on the nearest chairs, shouting, "Chi Hai, Chi Hai." Boaz chomped on his dinner in the cool breezes of the balcony while we ate inside, sweltering in the heat.

Another time one of the visiting ministers, Herb Hewitt, the union educational secretary, graciously emptied our cat's litter box, filling it with fresh dirt which he himself had brought from the garden downstairs. Ruthita and I will revere him eternally.

So much more I recall about our life together. Humor

continually surrounded us. It sounds as though all we did was play. But we sandwiched our fun into the eighteen-hour workdays as carefully as possible, often abandoning sleep in the process.

Ruthita returned to Union College several months before my term ended. I wept as her jet swooped up into the skies above Vietnam. Life was empty without her.

My Guardian Angel Works Overtime

Once again the late afternoon shadows lengthened across the compound. I trudged back down the dusty path from the apartment to my office, where more piles of work lay waiting for me. My body half ached with fatigue from a long day's work already, so the prospect of several more hours in my office that particular evening didn't especially thrill me.

Piles of large crates of military-donated equipment for the proposed new Adventist hospital plus heaps of cement and steel dotted the lawn and lined the path. The shadows around them seemed eerie and even menacing. Suddenly bizarre noises erupted from the towering wooden crates. Raucous scratching and scraping followed a hissing. Then an ominous silence pervaded the compound. I stopped and glanced upward to investigate. At that moment I heard a loud Eek! then loud laughter. Instantly the nimble forms of two teen-age girls jumped down beside me from their concealed perches on the crates. Cherie and Kathy, whose parents were missionaries in Saigon, were home from Far Eastern Academy in Singapore for summer vacation. The girls quickly grabbed my office keys from my fingers and dashed around one of the monstrous crates. Playfully I started chasing them to retrieve the keys.

"Now just what do you think you girls are trying to prove by stealing my precious keys?" By then I had reclaimed and grasped them firmly in my hands. The three of us sat down on the grass under one of the palm trees. A gentle breeze ruffled our hairdos, but we didn't mind. It had been a hot day, and we welcomed the coolness. Since the girls were gone most of the school year, we had not had an opportunity to become well acquainted, so now we sat chatting happily.

"Marilyn, when can you take us on a helicopter ride?" they asked eagerly, their eyes sparkling with excitement.

"What made you think I own helicopters so that I can take you riding?" I wrinkled up my nose and glared at them in mock sarcasm.

"Oh, you know what we mean. You know how to get chopper rides. Anyway, nobody else on the mission has begun to have as many as you have. They even land on the compound for you."

"That happened only twice, so don't get funny ideas. But right now I've got lots of work to do in the office. I don't have time to take you out to Ton Son Nhut. But I'll tell you what to do: just go to the helicopter control tower at the base and tell the operators you want a chopper ride, and they'll get you on."

"No," they responded, "our folks would never let us go out there without you. Besides, you work too much. That's why we stole your keys."

"I know, I know. But I've got so much work to do. Miss Atteberry from the division is coming soon to inspect the school, and I have to have things ready. She was the dean of the nursing school when I was a student, and I'm scared." But inwardly I longed for an excuse to escape the waiting pile of papers on my desk, and the thought was written all over my face. So the girls kept cajoling until they persuaded me to take them.

"But remember, it's getting toward dusk," I said finally. "We might have a hard time getting a ride since most of the chopper missions are in the morning. And we'll have to walk out to the base because the mission pickups are in use. Go find Ruthita and see if she wants to go. She hasn't had a chopper ride yet either." I caught their enthusiasm myself as I scurried upstairs to change into slacks. The office with its mountains of work I had totally forgotten.

So we dashed out the compound gate and headed toward Ton Son Nhut Air Base by foot. It wasn't long till a jeep driver stopped and asked our destination. He assured us he was also aimed toward Ton Son Nhut and offered us a ride. We all piled into the jeep's back seat, spilling out the open sides.

The jeep jerked to a quick halt at the gate, and the driver mechanically handed his identification pass to the guard.

"OK, girls. Here you are, but where were you planning to go on the air base? The theater? There are some good shows on tonight." The driver turned around and smiled broadly.

"Hotel Number Three [the military colloquial term for the heliport], if you don't mind, sir." My voice faltered sheepishly, noticing the you've-got-to-be-crazy expression on his face.

One seldom saw four American girls walking down the streets of Saigon. It was even more infrequent for them to fly around in helicopters. But I must admit that chopper riding was one of my favorite Vietnam pastimes, not that my busy schedule allowed much time for it.

Dutifully the driver dropped us at the heliport. The operations office had already closed for the day, so we climbed the control tower to inquire about helicopter rides. The GI's manning the tower welcomed us warmly. After we stated our desires, the tower operators commenced at once to radio the already airborne crafts, since no new missions were scheduled.

"Calling all helicopters . . . four American dames want a ride this afternoon." Our request sailed out into the skies around Saigon. The beeping and crackling sounds of the communications system produced an instant answer, not fully decipherable to our civilian ears but duly interpreted by the experts assisting us.

An answer came: "Must make a hop to Bien Hoa. . . . Tell the dames to meet us on the heliport in five minutes . . . Chopper 508 Big Red Baron."

"We're really going to get a ride tonight?" Kathy shouted. The faces of my three helicopter-riding novices nearly exploded with excitement. An intangible warmth flowing through my body reminded me my face wasn't exempt from an exuberant expression either.

"Thanks so much, you guys. You'll never know how we appreciate this," we all chimed in together. "We're Seventh-day Adventist missionaries. If you ever want a home-cooked meal, come to our mission servicemen's center on Cach Mang on Saturdays," we added hastily as we nearly jumped down the six flights of steel steps from the control tower. Arriving safely on the pavement under the tower, we waved a quick good-bye and dashed madly out toward the landing area. We rushed by rows of empty green choppers, their usually whirring rotors now still—all waiting side by side for new missions in the morning. Some of the helicopters were tiny, almost delicate objects, called loches. In sharp contrast squatted giant Chinooks—ugly hunks of green or camouflaged metal, splashed with a hodgepodge of round porthole-type windows. They reminded me of many-eyed monsters—half elephant, half caterpillar. Then we passed a multitude of an in-between-sized craft—the most common helicopters—called Hueys.

By now 508 Big Red Baron had landed, setting its spindly legs on the Ton Son Nhut turf. The rotors whirred raucously, tossing our freshly combed tresses as we ran to the helicopter. Ruthita had worn a wig with long hair, and she ran along with one hand on her head valiantly fighting to keep it in place. Ordinarily the rest of us would split with laughter over her predicament, but our jubilance over the forthcoming flight kept us strangely silent.

"Watch your step, girls," the gunner shouted, hopping down from his open seat in the rear of the helicopter beside the machine gun. He gave us a hand in climbing up into the craft. "Go right on over to the other side, each of you take a seat, and fasten your belts tight. The pilot likes to leave the sides open," he shouted above the deafening roar of the motor.

"Thank you," we yelled back.

After we belted in, the pilot, sitting directly in front of us, turned and grinned broadly. "Welcome aboard. What are four young American ladies like you doing in Vietnam?" he screamed.

"We're missionaries." Being so accustomed to the question, we automatically yelled back in unison.

With that, the pilot nodded his head, pulled a black-handled lever, adjusted some knobs, and instantly the craft surged upward, then sprinted sideways with a jerk, hovering momentarily while the copilot conversed with the control tower for final clearance. Suddenly the chopper lunged forward, then effortlessly lifted itself high into the air, leaving Ton Son Nhut behind us in a windy blur. We soared above the green rice paddies beneath us, and as the pilot banked sharply to the left, it seemed almost as though the paddies jumped up to meet us. The setting sun reflected itself in burnished gold hues in the little irrigation ditches that crisscrossed the paddies.

Military helicopter riding was so much more scenic than regular air travel because of the view through the open sides—if the pilot cooperated. The turns and banks sent the land scrambling to meet the sky at odd angles. It was like being on a wild rollercoaster or similar exciting amusement park ride. Sometimes the chopper skimmed over the paddies and villages, flirting with the palm tree branches. Then the metal bird instantly changed direction and floated upward to heights of several thousand feet where one could view the total landscape below. As we whizzed on, I glanced over at the girls and noticed a happy glow emanating from their faces, and I knew immediately we all shared identical feelings about helicopter riding.

We landed at Bien Hoa Air Force Base about forty miles from Saigon. The crew attended to the business that had brought the helicopter to the base while the pilot took us to the officers' dining area as his guests. We sat sipping our 7ups while our host interrogated us about our presence in Vietnam. Being American women in Vietnam offered many opportunities to witness for the church in that people were always asking us why we were there. We explained in detail about our Seventh-day Adventist mission and the work we did. He knew about the hospital and told us the glowing reports he had heard about it.

"I understand that it is the best civilian hospital in the country," he stated. Then he related how he wished his life had been more productive in terms of service to others and how he actually envied us as missionaries.

The crew attended to their assigned army business promptly. Soon the helicopter soared upward into the night sky and headed toward Saigon, its contented passengers buckled within. The return flight was uneventful except that when it started raining, the crew closed the sliding doors. The raindrops glistened on the windows in the moonlight. The uniqueness of the situation—riding a helicopter in a monsoon downpour, entranced by the beauty of the moonlight—fascinated me. I felt a warmth of contentment and gratefulness within. It felt good to be alive. Before long the helicopter touched earth once again. The four of us made our way home safely with the assistance of another set of military benefactors who cheerfully deposited us within the confines of the mission wall by way of their army truck.

Waving to my three companions, I walked toward my office. Suddenly I heard the voice of a doctor's wife calling, "Marilyn, Marilyn." I turned around and walked over to the porch where she stood. The concerned expression on her face was visible in the faint shimmer of moonlight peeking through the trees.

"Were you and the girls out helicopter riding this evening?" she questioned, almost sternly. Furrows creased her brow.

"Yes, we just got back from a short run to Bien Hoa. We've been gone only a couple of hours. Was there something you needed while I was gone?" My hesitant answer stuck in my throat. Suddenly slight twinges of guilt mingled with irritation welled up inside me, but I quenched them quickly. There was nothing wrong with an innocent helicopter ride once in a while, I told myself. After all, I just wasn't the type of person who could remain penned up for long periods of time and still produce efficiently. Why couldn't an individual ever have any privacy? My thoughts must have revealed themselves on my face.

"Oh, I didn't mean to interfere. It is just that the doctor and I were worried about you. Just about five minutes ago we received the report that twenty minutes earlier four army helicopters were shot down between Ton Son Nhut and Bien Hoa. You must have just barely escaped." Her anxious expression intensified. "How long have you been on the ground now?"

I glanced down at my watch, straining to see the hands in the semidarkness. "Exactly twenty minutes; but I didn't hear any fighting. The roar of the motors, though, makes it impossible to hear, and since it was raining, the sides were closed so I didn't see anything———" For a second I couldn't say anything. Then I blurted out, "Why, we must have flown right over it."

"Yes, you must have. Listen! Can't you hear the machine guns over in that direction right now?" The older woman's eyes filled with a tenderness that completely softened the furrows in her brow. She stood silently for a long moment. I wondered if she would scold me. Then she spoke slowly and deliberately, a loving tenderness in her voice as she added, "Marilyn, your guardian angel really works overtime."

Saigon Sabbaths

Sabbaths in Vietnam didn't exactly give us missionaries a respite from our busy schedules, but they did refresh us in their own unique manner. I looked forward to Sabbaths because they were always different. For one thing, it was exciting to see how many GI's could make it in for church—just to learn if we'd fixed enough food for them. Then many times on weekends visitors passed through—missionaries assigned to other places who stopped off in Saigon for the weekend—so I was always eager to see who might turn up. Such interesting individuals arrived: people from Europe, missionaries from India, students from the Middle East.

The Vietnamese members had their own Sabbath School, and we who spoke English had our separate study. Afterward we joined together for church to listen to the translated sermon. In time, each group had its own service.

The Adventist churches in Saigon had several interesting programs going on in the area in which we missionaries participated as well. For example, we received permission to conduct religious services at a large Viet Cong prison about thirty miles out of Saigon. So every Sabbath morning the red mission pickup truck drove out to it loaded with those providing special music, the Sabbath School teachers, and speakers for the sermon. The little chapel had a pump organ, and the prisoners loved to sing. The mission had been evangelizing the prisoners for a couple of years and had baptized about thirty. Some Sabbaths the attendance swelled to six hundred.

When we arrived at the prison, the Vietnamese guards led us through several sets of locked doors and mazes of barbed wire until we arrived at the meeting place. Then all the black-pajamaed prisoners had to stand at attention as we marched through them to the front of the building under a banner of South Vietnamese flags. Such fanfare always embarrassed me just a bit. Why couldn't we just simply slip in the back or the sides without the escort? After all, we were all equal—prisoners, missionaries, and Vietnamese. As time passed, more prisoners requested baptism. The baptisms were quite ceremonious, complete with distinguished Vietnamese official guests, more flags, and more flourish. Such ostentatious display certainly was not our desire, but God must have understood.

The trip to the prison was always exciting. We had to pass two large U.S. military posts circled by miles of barbed wire. Sometimes we got caught in the military traffic, hemmed in by tanks, armored personnel carriers, and long convoys of gigantic army trucks, not to mention the dozens of jeeps. A few times I made the trip on the back of one of the Vietnamese minister's motorcycles, clutching my clarinet tightly with one hand and holding onto the belt of my driver with the other as we sped in and around the convoys and buses. Once we traversed the highway just a little while after a battle. Mortar shells and cartridges littered the whole road. With charred vehicles and disheveled bushes and trees lining the roadsides, the surrounding area showed evidences of the early morning attack.

One Sabbath morning our compound guest was Miss Atteberry, the nursing consultant for the Far Eastern Division, who had come to help me develop senior-year course outlines.

She had been my dean of nursing in school, and I had regarded her with great trepidation until I discovered that she was human as well. Since it was my turn to drive the pickup out to the prison with the Vietnamese Sabbath speakers, I invited her to join me. All went well the first few miles, but suddenly trouble brewed as several small puffs of smoke steamed from the engine. Gingerly I maneuvered the vehicle off to the side of the road beside rolls of barbed wire. Neither passengers nor I knew the slightest bit about motors. But instantly two truckloads of GI's stopped behind our pickup and began investigating the difficulty.

Meanwhile my guest stood off in the shade behind one of the army trucks, since the day was starting to get hot by then. One of the men sitting in the back of the truck suddenly looked up and saw her there, her white hair glistening in the morning sun. He sat almost spellbound. Then his deep voice broke the silence as he stated respectfully, "My, it is good to see an American woman!" I believe she will treasure those words as one of her favorite recollections of the Orient.

Since the truck was unrepairable at that time or place, the GI's pushed it into the courtyard of a nearby military camp for safekeeping until one of the mission men could attend to its mechanical problems. My guest and I found a ride back into Saigon with a jeep while the Vietnamese hitchhiked on to the prison for the morning appointment.

From time to time the government released the converted VC's and allowed them to go home. One little wispy-bearded man was among the lucky few to find liberation. He was eager to get home to the central highlands and share his newfound joy in Christ with his family. But upon his return to the home village, he found that his wife and family had all died in the war several months before. Heartbroken, he returned to our mission in Saigon. Here he started piecing together fragments of his shattered life by involving himself in the various church activities and working for the hospital as gatekeeper. Every morning he smiled as he opened the iron gates for me. Sometimes I almost wanted to run, throw my arms around him, and whisper, "God bless you, dear man. You put me to shame. You've been through so much and can still be so cheerful."

Then another VC convert returned to his hamlet just south of Saigon, where he enthusiastically started a Branch Sabbath School. It eventually became a church. Over twenty had been baptized when I later left Vietnam. Since the Sabbath School was located in an "insecure" area, we Americans visited the village infrequently to avoid any possible harassment that could have resulted had we attended regularly. The Vietnamese believers went weekly to help, however.

Another Saigon Sabbath activity involved trips to a large Buddhist orphanage, with nearly two thousand homeless children, situated about twenty-five miles from Saigon. Every Sabbath afternoon the mission truck, loaded up with storytellers, song directors, and musicians, headed to what became known as the world's largest Branch Sabbath School. We divided children into smaller groups according to age, and the church members would tell them the love of Christ. The Buddhist leader of the orphanage welcomed us warmly as a result of the immunization program our hospital conducted for the children. He asked us to return week after week with the stories, songs, clarinets, accordions, and violins that we amateurs provided. The children charmed us with their appreciation. In my memory's ear I can still hear their high voices ring out with "Jesus Loves Me" in Vietnamese—children in a Buddhist orphanage singing Christian songs.

I loved to wander up and down the rows of thatch-roofed buildings that comprised the orphans' village, just looking at all the children. The long building housing all the infants is where I spent much of my time. Some of the babies showed signs of mixed parentage as evidenced by black kinky hair, or big blue eyes contrasted against their light brown skins. At times they looked so pathetic I wanted to cry, especially as I thought about the emotional trauma that some must have gone through. The battles might separate children from their parents so that they never find one another again. Then the authorities would gather up the children and bring them to the numerous orphanages that dotted Vietnam. No doubt some of the other children had watched their parents die. Many had living mothers or fathers too poor to feed and clothe them.

The children always appeared spotless in their saffron robes and shaved heads. When they passed a visitor, they bowed respectfully. Even after receiving the painful immunizations, they bowed politely to us nurses while the tears streamed down their faces.

Several hundred adults, dressed similarly to Buddhist nuns and priests, took care of the children. During the Bible story hour for the children, our Vietnamese Adventists held a Bible class for the adult caretakers. On one occasion we gave two hundred Voice of Prophecy Bible course certificates to the group. We were all grateful to God for that breakthrough.

This orphanage was located in an area the military termed "insecure." Sometimes fighting took place in the area, but Sabbath afternoons somehow seemed peaceful, though we could frequently hear the sounds of battle in the near distance. At times the enemy must have come quite close, because we could watch small American bombers strafing the countryside just across the road from the orphanage, and helicopter gunships flew in formation overhead. Many times the ground rumbled and trembled from the explosions around us. Yet we traveled safely to and from Saigon each Sabbath afternoon. We were quite certain that God was sending special protection for us.

One afternoon I well remember that we stayed later than

usual, and dusk was gathering as we slipped into the VW bus to start for home. As we jerked along the rutty road I noticed a tank grinding along beside us, its huge cannon pointed forward in the direction we headed. The gunner was not firing at us, but I can still feel the chills running up my spine as I recall its pounding blasts. In one way the scene was picturesque with the brilliant red flashes silhouetted against the dark horizon. It didn't feel beautiful, though, because other battle sounds started looming around us. The occupants of our vehicle were truly thankful to arrive home safely that evening.

At another time an explosion blew up a concrete bridge only minutes after our Adventist group had crossed it safely.

One Sabbath morning a missionary couple joined Ruthita and me on a helicopter trip to a base named Cu Chi where several Adventist servicemen were stationed. The fellows had been unable to leave their base to get into Saigon for quite a while, so we missionaries joined them in their little army chapel for worship and spent the day with them. That afternoon when we discovered no helicopters scheduled to return to Saigon, we hopped on a troop transport plane that just "happened" to be flying there.

Rows of junky bars lined the street just across from our compound gate. All day long, but especially at night, blaring rock music from them fought with the noise of air horns, choppers, and jets. From our mission we could see the soldiers wandering from one bar to another. One of the missionary wives became burdened for the host of Vietnamese girls who worked in them. She decided to put her convictions into practice Sabbath afternoons. Not wanting to enter the bars alone, she asked me to join her. We piled our arms with religious publications and marched across the street. I had never set foot in a bar in my life, so it was quite an adventure for me.

My knees shook with fright as we approached the first door.

I was supposed to hand out *These Times* and talk to the GI's while she spoke to the bar girls in her fluent Vietnamese. Her mission was quite successful. Mine was not. I couldn't think of one word to say to those men as I handed each a magazine. In the dimness of the eerie interiors, I felt grossly uncomfortable. The GI's gave me long half-starved stares with eyes that smoldered with lust. I was glad to leave. My calling was definitely not to minister to the American soldiers in the bars, I immediately decided.

Even though God was always near, sometimes I almost forgot He existed. Late one Friday afternoon I stood outside the compound gate, trying to catch glimpses of the setting sun. The week had been especially frustrating. The host of problems and enormous work load seemed to have doubled. It appeared every conceivable disaster that could transpire had. I felt as though my arms and legs were chunks of solid lead hanging from mere threads, and my mind resembled a big fuzzy blur. Physically and mentally I felt exhausted. The military trucks roared past. The choppers buzzed directly overhead. The jets from Ton Son Nhut Air Base screamed down from their lofty heights, while waves of rock music blared through the open doors of the bars across the street. The blatant uproar drenched my spirit with even more weariness.

I felt like shouting, "Shut up, you war. I want ten minutes of peace." Then to myself I hastened to add, "God, where are You? Your whole world is coming unglued . . . this dumb war . . . Your mission . . . God, just where are You? I can't reach You anymore. If this is what Your work is like, then forget it. I don't see any point to it."

The long shadows of the trees outside the compound gate stretched out to meet the confusion on the darkening street, telling me that sundown was almost here. Suddenly I wanted to forget about Sabbath, turn my back on the mission gates, walk off, and never come back. In a way I even wanted to forget about God. I felt that life was just too frustrating. As I stood alone in the dusty dusk, tears of bitterness, resentment, and utter fatigue streamed down my face.

Then strange feelings of peace filled me. I almost felt a still voice within me talking. "Marilyn, you must look beyond catastrophes, wars, organizations, or people to find Me. . . . I am still here, even in Vietnam. But I must let you humans do My work for the blessing it gives you. Please trust Me—don't let anything destroy our relationship. . . . I love you."

Silently I turned around, forced one foot ahead of the other, and went back in through the gate. I marched myself up to the old yellow mission house and climbed the gray cement stairs to my apartment. Staggering to my bedroom, I collapsed on my knees beside my bed and let the tears flow. For a long time I sobbed alone in the darkness. Finally I cried out, "O God, help me. Why am I here? Sometimes I hate it . . . I hate the war . . . I hate the responsibilities. . . . It's too much . . . I'm too disorganized . . . I'm not smart enough . . . I'm not strong enough . . . I can't stand it. And, dear God, . . . the missionaries . . . well, sometimes we just don't understand each other. I make them mad, and they accuse me of things I haven't done. . . . What's wrong? . . . well . . . oh, I'm just too weak. I feel as though the most horrible parts of my personality have suddenly been flaunted before the whole universe . . . ugly stuff is coming out of me that I never dreamed was there. . . . What have You done to me, God?"

The still small voice within me seemed to answer again, "I understand. I know it's hard. But for right now think about the pleasant aspects of your life. . . . You have health, food, clothes, a comfortable place to live. Look at those poor people outside your compound wall. . . . Many don't have food or a place to sleep. And remember your favorite quotation?

" 'God never leads His children otherwise than they would

choose to be led, if they could see the end from the beginning, and discern the glory of the purpose which they are fulfilling as coworkers with Him.'

"I'm still here, child. I'll give you strength."

"Yes, God, I know. Sometimes I blame this war and everything on You. But it isn't Your fault. How can I be so stupid? Please help me. Please forgive me."

A quiet tranquillity filled me. I was at peace once again. If only I had let God's Spirit soften me more and allowed Him to give me more understanding and forgiveness. I felt safe in His gracious forgiveness for my frailties and weaknesses.

Sometimes I longed for a quiet, restful Sabbath in some peaceful place. But even though jets and choppers continuously screeched overhead and air horns shattered the air, Sabbaths still held a special sacredness that separated them from the other days. Sometimes on Sabbaths I just stayed in my apartment to read or listen to my tapes of sacred music, bathing my soul in serenity. Those were cherished moments when I could stop and try to listen to God. I learned many lessons on Sabbaths in Saigon.

"Nice Knowing You, 'Nam"*

"Air Vietnam announces the departure of its flight 816 to Singapore . . ." The soft French-accented voice droned on over the loudspeaker. Waving a quick good-bye to my friends who had escorted me to the airport, I walked silently toward the waiting jet out on the runway.

A gentle misty rain fell on Saigon's Ton Son Nhut airport, making the red, green, and blue runway lights twinkle and sparkle in the dusk. The soft sounds of music from a GI's radio floated through the moist air. I happened to catch the melody as I hastened by. There it was—"my song." The lyrics rushed through me as waves of emotion engulfed me until I found myself almost running along the airfield toward my jet to escape the memories the song unearthed. The words pounded through me: "Raindrops keep falling on my head . . . but that doesn't mean my eyes will soon be turning red . . . crying's not for me . . ."

On the Saigon compound my theme song at times could well have been: "Nobody knows the trouble I've seen," but I'd adopted "Raindrops" in an attempt to produce a stoic bravery within myself that was not naturally there. It had not worked entirely, and at that moment I didn't want to be reminded of it.

*A nickname the GI's gave Vietnam.

Just a few tears, mingled with the soft drops from the sky, trickled down my face while my feet stumbled mechanically up the ramp into the 727 cabin. I slipped into my assigned window seat and quickly fastened the safety belt. Brushing the dampness from my cheek, I stared at the blurred lights of Saigon as the jet lifted gently into the darkness of the Oriental night. As I sank back into my seat, memories of the past two years flooded over me. Some were sad, some angry, yet many were fond. In my mind's eye I saw the forty nursing students lining the road to the compound gate, waving to me as the airport-bound vehicle in which I sat inched its way past the sobbing girls. That was less than an hour ago. Now here I was on the plane. Sitting up straight again, I turned my face toward the window, staring out into the black empty space beyond. I felt a mixture of sadness, weariness, relief, and frustration, coupled with joy.

"It will be good to be out of Vietnam," I told myself, settling back into my seat; yet my emotions continued to war mysteriously within. A slim, short Oriental stewardess glided gracefully up the aisle, the tail of her turquoise *ao dais* sailing behind her. Her long black hair fell smoothly to her waist. My eyes rested on her momentarily.

Suddenly the jet lunged into a quick bank to the left, jolting me back into the reality of the present. Then as it gently leveled off, my mind continued to deliberate. The delicate Vietnamese stewardess appeared with dinner. I watched her balance the trays skillfully as she steadied herself against the motion of the plane. Seeing her reminded me of my beautiful nursing students. I loved them. Remembering my nursing students made me recall the people of Vietnam. I really admired them. They possessed some truly noble qualities that seemed to shine above the poverty of their war-torn land. Sadly I realized what a privilege working with them and knowing them had been. The Vietnamese tolerated much pain and suffering, lived bravely under hard circumstances. Their patience and uncomplaining spirit had left an indelible impression on my mind. Memories of families huddled together in culverts, trying to find some covering from the monsoon downpours, flashed across my mind. The culverts were home after explosions had demolished their own dwellings. More pictures kept pouring into my mind—bodies lying along the roadside after a battle; little children crawling on the streets because their legs had been amputated after some war-related injury. Certainly I would never have reason to grumble. Vietnam had been a blessing to me.

I knew I cared about Vietnam and its people, but—— My thoughts buzzed on. At the same time I also knew that I wasn't the same person who had stepped off another Air Vietnam jet exactly two years before. My mind still churned with memories of recent frustrations and problems. Would I ever be able to really say, "Lord, I'll go where You want me to go"? I asked myself.

My mission term in Saigon had not been the type of experience that one could evaluate totally in positive superlatives. People told me that I'd encountered more problems in my two years in Saigon than most missionaries have in twenty years. So it had not been a completely joyful two-year period, and I viewed it with mixed feelings. From a logical standpoint, I had been too young to be dropped into the middle of the problems facing me. The administrative responsibilities and other burdens had weighed heavily on me, leaving me with a half-crushed, totally exhausted, life-has-passed-me-by-nobody-cares feeling. In some ways I felt like an old woman who has witnessed decades of life at its roughest. As I sat in my seat, waves of bitterness and cynicism toward life in general enveloped me—perhaps from the exposure of my youthful idealism to the war and the church and compound conflicts. But I determined to conquer

such negative feelings, given time. At the moment, though,
I would have been totally dishonest had I expounded in
glowing terms: "Wow, what a cool time I had in Saigon.
Mission life is really the greatest!"

Even so, here I sat, alive, strong, a survivor both
emotionally and physically. I thought of the many times I'd
inwardly called out, "Help! What do I do now?" Yet the answer
had always come. God had looked after me. He had given me
wisdom far beyond what I ever imagined possible. In fact, He
had blessed the efforts of all us missionaries. As a result I had
learned to have a greater trust in my heavenly Father. Because
He knows what He is doing when He directs His children, I
must be willing to go again. Yet, inwardly, I fought such
thoughts. No mission service for me, I told myself—never
again.

As I stared out into the darkness on that plane ride from
Saigon, I decided that I would not go home to the United States
even though my term had now ended—not until I had resolved
the bulk of my cynicism and bitterness. I could not stand up
and honestly tell mission reports with the negative feelings
toward the church I felt surging within—whether or not I ever
planned to return to overseas service.

In a way, I had shoved God to a back corner of my mind
because I felt He'd deserted me at times. I knew I had to
reacquaint myself with Him before I went home. Once more I
must be willing to fulfill His plan for my life, must be willing to let
Him lead me, though right now I fought the idea.

Sometimes we humans are strange creatures. Though I
wanted freedom from my unhappy thought patterns, I treasured
some of the bitterness and relished juicy bits of self-pity.
Actually I felt my final straw of disenchantment involved
ingratitude. Inwardly I nurtured hurt feelings because now as I
left, three full-time individuals would take over the work I had
struggled with by myself. Furthermore, the "establishment" and

"organization" had not expressed appreciation for my efforts. I'd seen the letters of thanks the student missionaries had received from the various union and division administrators on completion of their assignments, and had heard the leaders give speeches of gratitude—but I received no such letters or speeches and I even wept with envy before I left Saigon when I realized my replacements could sleep till six in the morning when I had frequently risen at two o'clock to get the work done. Furthermore, life was more peaceful now, and the compound conflict had quieted.

I should have been happy that they wouldn't have some of the problems I'd faced. The school needed all the help it could get. The students needed to learn things I hadn't had time to teach, and the curriculum needed the polish I hadn't had the training or experience to give. Besides, my replacements would encounter the problems my administration bequeathed. My condolences should have gone out to them.

But instead, I sat basking in my discontent and sheer bitterness. I just didn't have the maturity, Christian grace, or emotional energy to rise above myself right then. Vietnam had given me a crash course in growing up, and I feared I had flunked. I was angry—I hadn't failed anything in my life yet; why start now? Pervading the other negative feelings surging within were the thoughts that my church had completely taken advantage of me, draining the last ounce of energy from my spirit and body without appreciation. So I promised myself the luxury of home only after I'd decided just what to do with my negative attitude. My parents must not see me now, I told myself. It would hurt them deeply. I loved them too much to bring them such pain.

But God patiently bore with me, watching over me tenderly. I reminded myself of Jonah sulking on the outskirts of Nineveh after God had helped him accomplish his assignment. And my heavenly Father lovingly provided for my psychological comfort just as surely as He gave Jonah the physical shade of that vine.

I volunteered as a jungle nurse for the Sarawak Mission on the island of Borneo while I sorted through my feelings on Vietnam and mission service with God. So I held clinics, sewed up lacerations, delivered babies, and gave immunizations in the villages along the rivers deep in the jungle interior, loving every minute. Also I gave primitive health education lectures and held Branch Sabbath Schools. I worked hard during the day, and when night came I was exhausted physically, yet sleep would not come. As a result I spent hours in the darkness talking to God while the tropical moon shimmered overhead.

They were not always gentle, subdued conversations with my Maker, for many times I spoke to Him almost harshly. My angry soul nearly burst with resentment toward my church and some of its prescribed ways, the world, and the inconsistency of its wars, and Him—why did He allow all this mess so long? Yet I begged for inner peace. I pleaded for a forgiving spirit toward my co-workers and for freedom from jealousy. Then I asked for an inner stamina that could rise above the seeming ingratitude for my work, and for release from my anger toward the church in general. There was that same cry: "Please help me, God. What do I do now?" God listened and answered. The serenity came and completely filled me. Forgiveness subdued my sour spirit. Little by little a flicker of confidence exposed itself quietly within and softly whispered, "Marilyn, you did the best you could under the circumstances—no one ever needs to thank you for anything you do as long as *you* know that. You're too strong to let such insignificant matters overpower you." So I emerged from those jungles with a whole new personality evolving. Once again I could accept life as it is; once again I was willing to work to make the world a better place. Now, with God's help, that sensitivity I'd always felt for myself could be pulled out to be directed toward others.

A certain dash of adventure gallops within me. When my volunteer duty on Borneo ended, I jaunted all over Asia, North Africa, the Middle East, Europe, and South America before I allowed my travel-weary spirit to taste the joys of the civilized life of my homeland. I had visited seventy-eight countries of the globe—explored my planet—and in so doing visited Adventist missions all over the world. And I'd discovered that Vietnam and even Marilyn Bennett didn't have a monopoly on earth's problems by any means.

Now I was on my last flight home. The jet descended toward Dallas. As usual the soft, even voice of the announcer droned on, "Thank you for flying American Airlines. You will be landing in five minutes. Passengers disembarking please use the forward doors."

Excitement welled up inside me. I would see my parents in just a few minutes. Yet a quiet happiness within loomed even greater than the anticipation of rejoining my family.

I could face life squarely with a "you-can't-defeat-me" attitude. I had fought an inner battle over bitterness and cynicism—and won. Once again I could laugh and mean it from the depths of my soul. And once again I could look out to the world and say, "Life, you are good; it's great to be alive."

God had started to teach me how to cope with life's problems. I felt humble and grateful that He had allowed me to encounter such a wide gamut of experiences early in life, because I could see where tremendous growth had taken place within me. As a result of my encounters with God, I could continue to face life victoriously. The negative feelings had vanished—He had taken them away. A gentle confidence and sweet serenity, softened by a deep satisfaction with life and a willingness to trust everything to my Maker, now filled me. Finally I had no doubt as to what my decision in regard to future mission service would be. Yes, I would be willing to go again someday if God needed me. My favorite quotation again focused clearly in my consciousness: "God never leads His children otherwise than they would choose to be led . . ."

Yes, I would have chosen Vietnam—even had I known what I would face. Thanks to my mission experience there, I was arriving home more assured and composed, an adult woman far more content with life and in tune with myself than I had been when I left Dallas a part-child three years earlier. I could honestly say, "Thank You, God, for Vietnam. Thank You for being able to use me. Thank You for the lessons." The work God accomplishes on earth, considering some of the tools He works with—like myself, for example—amazed me. I felt good about myself and the transformation He had effected within me.

By now the jet had landed. Passengers started unfolding from their seats and walking down the aisle toward the forward exit. I picked up my black travel-worn purse, tossed its strap over my shoulder, and marched toward the waiting lounge with an inner triumph—a triumph that only God fully understood.

There at the entrance stood my exuberant parents. I rushed on, throwing myself into their waiting arms. My father rubbed his masculine cheek against mine as he planted his kiss. Then his deep voice echoed around me as he almost shouted in his excitement, "Welcome home, baby!"

Epilogue

Even though I'd conquered the bulk of my negative feelings before I returned home, still on occasion I found myself declaring, "Never again." Then my conscience would stir, and I'd take my unhappy memories back to God. Together we'd work them through until a peace filled me, and I'd quietly say to my Maker, "Anywhere You lead—even Vietnam."

Because I own a personality that thirsts for the newness of tomorrow and doesn't dwell forever on past events, Vietnam eventually slipped away into the backseat of my memories.

But when I heard that the United States Army had lent the well-equipped Third Field Army Hospital to the church until the completion of the new Adventist hospital, I was excited. It seemed too good to be true. Fantastic Third Field in "our" possession? Then the Loma Linda University School of Medicine began rotating faculty members with Saigon Adventist Hospital. In time the LLU heart team went out, returning with glowing reports that it was their most successful overseas trip. Since I'd gone to Loma Linda to pursue graduate education, I heard firsthand news of the medical progress in Saigon as the various doctors came back. Sometimes my friends passed on to me comments they'd heard from the returning physicians: "The nurses in Saigon are great." "Some of the most efficient nurses I've ever worked with . . ." At times

I couldn't believe my ears and felt sure my friends were making up stories until the doctors would tell me the same things themselves.

But as I found myself caught up in the busy routine of graduate study, hospital work, and social life, thoughts of Saigon once again settled to a far corner of my mind.

Then suddenly I started hearing reports of Communist victories in Vietnam. When the northern section of South Vietnam fell, I felt stunned. It seemed too terrible to be true—yet it was happening right before my eyes as I viewed the events on TV. Danang fell during Easter vacation. I went to Santa Monica beach with one of my friends that Sunday. Although I tried to appear happy and pleasant, the vivid reality of the impending death of a nation I deeply cared about hung over me like a gray cloud. As I watched my fellow Americans playing so carefree around me—laughing, shouting, singing along with the radios beside them on the sand—I questioned silently, "Why is it that I have such a tranquil life here while my Vietnamese friends are losing their freedom? How is it that all these people around me can be so happy?—South Vietnam is falling!" I wasn't particularly jubilant company for my friend that day—he didn't really understand either, though he listened patiently while I talked about Vietnam. But he hadn't lived there—he hadn't known the people.

More and more rapidly the closing scenes of South Vietnam etched themselves on the face of history. I couldn't keep up with the reports fast enough. Now I only remember the sadness that drenched me those last weeks. What about the people? I kept asking myself. What about my students? What will happen to my friends? Desperately I longed to go back to say Good-bye. I eagerly yearned to do something—but I couldn't. The emotionally excruciating experience of standing by watching but being unable to do anything perplexed me. At that point I almost felt willing to give my life if that would ensure freedom for that country. During this time people continually asked, "How do you feel, Marilyn?" All I could answer was, "Sad—terribly, terribly sad."

Fleeting memories dashed through my mind. I had watched med-evac helicopters land one after another on the helipads beside various U.S. Army hospitals. I'd seen my moaning countrymen whisked away on stretchers, and I'd ask myself, Why? Why? When no answer came, I'd just quietly muse, "Oh, how thankful I am that my brother Jody isn't here." Then a flood of other war-linked thoughts involving both the Vietnamese and U.S. military filled my mind—memories of pain, deprivation, death, destruction, emotional excruciation, emaciation—all that, and still no freedom! Although I felt angry in thinking about what the war had done to alienate my own country within itself, feelings of sheer grief poured over me as I recalled Vietnam and its people. The utter futility of war overwhelmed my mind. A more intense longing for Jesus to return than I'd ever known before filled me.

Yet, amid the deep sadness within, I felt a contentment. A silent calm came from the knowledge that I'd done the best I could while there. Now I was glad I'd risen at 2 AM to do my work. The incongruity of sadness mingled with satisfaction mixed mysteriously within me. I could only vaguely recall the problems —I'd long ago forgiven both myself and my associates, and they in turn had forgiven me. Not so long ago I sat in the living room of one of them. We reminisced about some of our experiences. Suddenly my friend's voice grew soft and pensive as he added, "You know, Marilyn, I think the devil worked harder on our compound than anywhere else in Vietnam." I nodded. We embraced as I left.

Many accounts during those last days of Vietnam included Saigon Adventist Hospital—praises to the nursing care, praises to the dedicated physicians. I recall one of the last newscasts as the reporter extolled the institution. He went on to say that Saigon Adventist Hospital would go down in history as one of the few great legacies the Americans would leave in Vietnam. I again felt quiet surges of contentment in the knowledge that I'd had a small part in it.

In no way did I feel that I had wasted my two years of blood, sweat, and tears as the country changed governments. The nurses that Saigon Adventist Hospital helped to educate could continue to be a blessing under any regime. The people in Vietnam would remain the same—with identical needs. Though I staunchly oppose communism philosophically, I cannot hate people. I cannot wish anyone pain or discomfort—that's why I hate war. But what we missionaries did in Vietnam would live as long as those nurses lived, even though the school died. No, I did not feel my service had been lost.

Furthermore, in looking back over the time since I'd left Vietnam, I saw positive changes in myself—changes directly attributable to my experience there. No longer did I go limping along when confronted with new challenges. I felt quite adequate to fulfill most requests, within reasonable professional and educational limits, of course. For example, I'd accepted the chairmanship of a twenty-five-member student-faculty committee on the Loma Linda University campus. On one occasion the committee hosted the General Conference president, its secretariat, the treasurers, and the deans of the various schools of the university. Acting as chairman, I felt no trepidation, after asking for God's guidance.

Then occasionally the Loma Linda Medical Center has asked me to do relief nursing supervision for the entire institution on evening and night shifts. At first I'd feel twinges of fright, realizing that the responsibility for the entire university hospital lay on me those eight hours. But I kept telling myself, "Remember what God did for you in Saigon—this will be okay too." And so I walked the halls with a quiet confidence I hadn't known in past years.

Twenty job offers—many of them involving administration—waited for me after I completed my graduate
study. Managing people is still something I don't relish. I shall
always prefer the role of an Indian to that of a chief, but being a
follower can now be my choice and not my only option,
because I know I can—if necessary—handle leadership with
God's help. There is no panic. While I still realize my
limitations, I can identify my strengths as well—something I
could not readily do before. Furthermore, no longer do I require
or even expect praise for everything I do. Accomplishing the
task itself can be a sufficient reward.

Through God's help I've grown. All my life I'd heard my
father pray, "Lord, send our children the experiences they need
to grow and develop into the kind of people You want them to
be so You can use them." Vietnam has been one of the
answers to his prayers.

Then the refugees arrived. Over four hundred Vietnamese
sponsored by the Seventh-day Adventist Church flocked to
Loma Linda during the evacuation program just prior to the fall
of Saigon. From a selfish viewpoint I was extremely happy to
see my old friends from Vietnam. But for them, my heart
ached. Yes, America is a wonderful country, and I love it dearly
because it is mine. But it was not their home, and the grief over
the loss of their country is something my America can never
make up to them no matter how hard it may try. So again the
conflicting emotions of joy and sadness mixed. But sadness
predominated.

The refugees included twenty-one of my former
students—now graduate nurses. The reunion was exciting.
Though I knew they would endure much loneliness and sorrow
separated from their families, they seemed happy to see me
again. Now they and many others were right here in Loma
Linda—four hundred plus in need of housing, clothing, and,
most of all, love and understanding. Loma Linda and

surrounding communities opened their arms to the refugees in a way that I'd never dreamed imaginable. For the first few days, the Vietnamese stayed in the gymnasium. Cots lined the basketball courts, and a huge circus tent pitched just outside on the ball field served as their dining room. The churches in the area brought truckloads of clothes for them. Then, when the four hundred had waited out the quarantine period, completed their physical exams, and finished necessary registration, they scattered all over the United States. Adventist communities from Portland, Oregon, to Orlando, Florida, welcomed them with jobs, housing, food, and other necessities. One of the Saigon pastors immediately went to work in the large refugee center at Camp Pendleton in southern California. He cared so much about the spiritual welfare of his fellow countrymen that he wanted to do something to help.

Many of the refugees stayed in California, not knowing where else to go. Homes all over the Loma Linda area accepted them. I found myself coming home with as many as twelve of my former students when they wanted to stay with someone they'd known before. America was a strange new land for them, and they needed every link with the past we could possibly give them. The School of Medicine faculty and others who had taken their turns in Saigon shared their homes, hearts, and bank accounts.

So here I was, in my last quarter of graduate school, with eight to twelve people living in my two-bedroom accommodation. Though I had mountains of schoolwork and odds and ends to finish up before graduation, plus a 180-page paper to write for a final project and now a houseful of refugees, I knew the Lord would see it all through—and of course He did. Even though I had to spend hours finding jobs, clothes, and finally more permanent living quarters and furniture for my "family," the Lord took care of my scholastic needs too. My teachers graciously helped by giving me extended deadlines, and I graduated with my master's degree in spite of the pandemonium at my house.

I love those people, and for once I really tried to forget myself in reaching out to them. Whenever the girls needed something, I'd take it to the Lord, and what they required invariably appeared—whether it was a red coat, money for food, an apartment, a specific job, or furniture. I was proud of the way they tried to adjust to our way of life. Naturally, though, every household that accepted the newcomers had problems—cultural misunderstanding, communication barriers, that sometimes erupted in unhappiness for all. Suddenly I became one of the resource people for the refugees and Americans, and therefore received calls day and night for advice. The whole thing amused me, for I certainly didn't claim to have answers.

In time, both Loma Linda University and Pacific Union College set up rehabilitation programs for the SDA-sponsored refugee nurses, and a large English school started at La Sierra. Little by little they are learning our ways and language.

That misty evening when I flew away from Saigon, I had felt sure my commitment to Vietnam had ended. Never in the farthest stretch of my imagination did I conceive of my Vietnamese students and friends coming to my country. And never did I think that I'd be working with them or teaching them again. But Loma Linda University School of Nursing asked me to teach on their faculty, to be an advocate for the Vietnamese students entering the school. They offered the Saigon graduate nurses special help toward preparing for the U.S. state board examinations. I had almost decided to go to Africa, but when Loma Linda's request came, after much prayer I felt God wanted me for the Vietnamese once again. I am happy to be able to help.

DATE DUE

OCT 0 8 2014			
NOV 2 1 2014			
NOV 0 9 2015			
NOV 2 8 2015			